Dear Tu,

Thank you for being such a blessing to our IHOP community.

Joy Matthews

# DEDICATION

I dedicate this book to Christian workers in the sex trade industry – a difficult, but much needed outreach ministry. They are truly our Lord's redeeming hands and feet to a hurting world.

# ENDORSEMENTS

Statistics tell us that sex is by far the most popular search term on the web. I'm challenging you -- if you struggle with porn -- to read this book and devour it. It may be a lifeline for you even if you feel like you're going down for the third time. If porn and out-of-control sexuality aren't your temptation then I encourage you to get a copy of this book for a friend who is struggling. There is hope for all. This book provides practical insight and a bright hope.

Mike Bickle
International House of Prayer
*www.ihopkc.org*

*Under the Covers – A Message of Hope* is a book that needed to be written. Sex trafficking is a subject that is becoming more open to the public through the attention given through media. Oftentimes the victimized women and children do not have a voice to cry out for themselves, and this book gives them a voice. But there is also another group of victims: the johns who purchase the prostitutes. I applaud the author for the courage to compile this book. It reveals the johns' redemptive story with both love and insight. Read this book. It will fill you with hope.

Patricia King
Speaker, author, television host, and media producer
Founder of XPmedia.com and Overseer of
Christian Services Association
*www.xpministries.com*

"We live in an era that has seen the widespread desacralization of sex, the commodification of women's sexuality, and the industrialization of lust. Our sanctity and our solidarity have been breached and we need a road map back to freedom and wholeness. Under the Covers accomplishes just that. I encourage this read for everyone who has experienced sexual brokenness."

Benjamin Nolot
CEO & Founder of Exodus Cry | Filmmaker
*www.exoduscry.com*
*www.nefariousdocumentary.com*

The word "Sex" excites and titillates. For many men it triggers a series of thoughts that lead to behaviors which have negative consequences. 'Sex' makes promises of intimacy but for many men, after climax, we are left feeling lonely, shameful, guilty, and sad. The consequences are huge on ourselves, our partners and on the other people with whom we have sex. Also affected are the porn stars we watch, society at large and the host countries to which we travel in search of sexual encounters. But it doesn't have to be like that. This book brings a message of hope even for those who have reached rock bottom. It shares a message of grace we don't deserve but can still experience and a God who deeply loves us. Read. Listen. Absorb. Believe."

Glenn Miles, PhD
International Child & Vulnerable Persons Rights Consultant
Co-editor with Christa Foster Crawford of 'Stopping the Traffick: A Christian Response to Sexual Exploitation & Trafficking' (Regnum 2014) *www.ocms. ac.uk/regnum*
*www.gmmiles.co.uk* for research and resources
*www.good-touch-bad-touch-asia.org* - prevention tool for school aged children.
*www.celebratingchildrentraining.* info basic training for faith based practitioners working with children at risk.

If you're struggling with porn, sex addiction or abuse, or if you were abused this way, then I encourage you to read this book. It gives hope, advice and a strategy to those who want to overcome sexual addiction of any kind. The book is full of helpful testimonies, practical advice and abundant references that point the way out of addiction for those desiring freedom. Read this book and begin allowing God to change your life.

Pastor Darrell Brazell
New Hope Fellowship
*www.NewHopeLawrence.com*
New Hope for Sexual Integrity
*www.NewHope4si.com*

Nothing speaks more powerfully to a person's pain and brokenness than the story of a fellow traveler, especially one who has walked a similar path and reached higher ground. Under the Covers is a powerful book that will connect with those longing for hope and a clearer picture of what healing looks like in real life.

If you are drowning in your brokenness, you are not alone; God has not forgotten about you, and a growing army of brothers and sisters stand ready to help you overcome. Our thanks to J. L. Matthews for producing such an invaluable resource.

Jonathan & Elaine Daugherty
Director and Radio Host
Be Broken Ministries
*www.bebroken.com*
*http://2.bebroken.com/about-us.html*
*www.puresexradio.com*


There are many people and ministries who are feeling the burden of the Lord's heart to bring healing and freedom to the masses who are being sexually abused and exploited --- but it's very unusual to find those who shine the light of Jesus into the *actual sex abuser's lives,* offering them healing and freedom too! J. L. Matthews' book *Under the Covers* is a treasure trove of keys that can unlock doors for those caught in the grips of the enemy's seductions. It is a heart-felt, nonjudgmental book of HOPE and encouragement for those who are trapped! Matthews' reveals root causes of sexual additions, shares marvelous testimonies from those who have been set free, and asks significant questions after each chapter to engage the reader in an honest, personal examination of their heart. Corrie ten Boom once said, "There is no pit so deep that God's love is not deeper still." Matthews engaging book trumpets genuine hope for anyone who longs for and is desperate to be free and clean to live real life again!

Linda Valen
*Ministry Director*
Master Potter Ministries
*www.masterpotter.com*


"Having worked with Christian men for over five decades, I have concluded that, whereas Christian men would agree that they are fully saved, they don't often agree that they are fully loved. The battle is with our preoccupation with sin management. Approaching life from a shame-based faith, we imagine balancing what they have done, where they have failed and sinned, through religious, ritual activities to off-set the balance beam of our brokenness. Kudos to this book for pointing out the long-term effects of abuse and addiction as well as giving hope in the finished work of the Cross. It calls men away from sin-management to a life of authentic faith and openness. It encourages us to embrace our nature, our abuse, our addictions and our past as we look through the eyes of God and how He has forgiven us in Christ and called us to live."

Gary Goodell
Third Day Churches International
"Permission Granted To Do Churches Differently in the 21st Century"
"Where Would Jesus Lead?"


As young men we grow up in a society that declares sex and sexuality to be one of the highest pursuits in life. Our society tells us there is virtually no right or wrong way to express our sexual thoughts and urges. We can desire the beautiful; we can pursue our sexual cravings almost without boundary. But our culture doesn't tell us these desires can grow darker and more twisted over time. No one tells us that once you're in, there's no way out of here. We soon find out just how powerful our sexual habits are as they start to consume us, control us, and even devour us inside. We realize how toxic we've become but we can't tell anyone now; the society that embraced us and our youthful fantasies now calls us sick, perverted, and dirty. Welcome to the new world. But is this all there is to say; is there no hope for men?

If you've picked up this book you may be wondering the very same thing. Is there hope for men like me or for my brother, my father, or my friend? The answer is a resounding YES; there is hope. There is a power far greater than your sexual desires, far greater than your habits and addictions. There is a God who loves you and wants to set you free, no matter how dark your thoughts may be. Read this book and listen to the voices of men and women who share their stories of pain and freedom as they struggle with the impact and destruction caused by pornography and sexual addictions. Read on and start to walk out the freedom you've longed for inside.

Todd Morrison
UntoLife
Mechanicsburg, PA
Phnom Penh, Cambodia

"So many men believe the lies: "She's too young to remember," or "It won't affect her." If only porn users understood how they rob themselves of true intimacy in marriage... if only fathers and grandfathers, brothers and cousins, uncles and neighbors knew the devastated lives they leave behind them for crossing the line just once, then our mental health system would not be so burdened, our marriages would suffer less, there would be fewer women who cut, rage, abuse drugs and alcohol, engage in eating disorders and more. Thank you for telling them that there is healing and forgiveness."

Dr. Lynda L. Irons
Founder and Director,
Clean Vessels Ministry, Inc.

# TABLE OF CONTENTS

## Section I    To Men, From Other Men on Their Journey

## Section II    From the Hearts of Women

## Section III    From Heaven's Eyes

## Section IV    A Man's Ultimate Destiny: A View from Heaven

## Appendix

# FOREWORD

Which of these words would you use to describe yourself or your life?

| | |
|---|---|
| A disaster | Unfulfilled |
| A disappointment | Emotionally numb |
| Depressed | Full of regret |
| Disgusted with yourself | Empty |
| Discouraged | Stuck |
| Frustrated with yourself | Hopeless |
| Just getting by | Lonely |
| Nobody really knows me | Rejected |

If you feel any of these words describe you, this book is for you. If you've done some things that have left you angry, frustrated, or disgusted with yourself, this book is for you.

Winston Churchill once said, "If you're going through hell, keep going." That's pretty good advice. You might feel like your life is hell or that you live in hell. But I want you to know that's untrue. There's still hope even if you can't see it.

This book is about people who have done some bad things and the consequences of their actions, but also about how they were able to leave that life behind for another life, a better one. They've been where you might be right now.

We're cheering for you, praying for you, and hoping that within the years to come  you can become all you are meant to be – someone who can lift their head up high and live without any regrets – a different person than you are now. If others can do it, you can too. This book can show you how. Please turn the page and keep reading.

"Why are you in despair, O my soul?
And, why have you become disturbed within me?
Hope in God.[1]"

Hal Linhardt
Director of Evangelism
IHOPKC
*www.IHOPKC.org*

# PREFACE

A wonderful team has been assembled to write this book especially with you in mind. We are grateful that you picked it up. The book is unique because it's specifically written to those who want to be free from porn, buying sex and to those who have been incarcerated for sexual offenses. It will also be a help if you experienced sexual abuse that still haunts you and drives you to exploit others. We want to tell you that no matter who you are, what you've done or how addicted you are, there is hope for you. No matter how many times you've tried and failed before, right now you hold in your hand the key to freedom.

We want to encourage you, share our love with you, and tell you about a relationship with Someone who will bring peace where there is only despair and Who will bring hope for a positive future.

This book also features stories from men who have successfully broken free of their addictions, stories from women to bring understanding of their experiences, and finally a message of hope and forgiveness to all men, who struggle with sexual issues as well.

> *Nobody can go back and start a new beginning,*
> *but anyone can start today and make a new ending.*

It's not an accident that you're holding this book now. Many have been praying that the right people would pick it up and benefit from it. The failures of yesterday or last month or the last ten years don't have to determine what the next ten years will look like. There is forgiveness, there is healing, and there is a brighter future than your past would indicate. Remember, "Nobody can go back and start a new beginning, but anyone can start today and make a new ending."[2] Today is your day.

# SECTION I

## To Men From Other Men On Their Journey

# PORNOGRAPHY
# MY DRUG OF CHOICE

My name is Bill Corum, and I am going to share some of my story of being addicted to pornography and prostitutes in hopes that it will help you. I have kept this part of my life buried for over 30 years, for two reasons. First, I was ashamed. Second, I didn't want to hurt my children.

In January of 2013 I wrote a book called *The Ultimate Pardon*, which revealed secrets I had kept hidden all those years. Since the book was published in August of 2013, I have given an interview for a documentary on pornography and being a sex abuser. I am contributing to this book with the hope that even one person who is addicted as badly as I was might find freedom.

My first exposure to pornography was in the early 1950s, somewhere between the ages of eight and ten. It was a little cartoon booklet. When I flipped the pages, the figures would move. It was like watching a movie, but with cartoon people performing the sex acts. About that same time, I started looking at Playboy; this was early in the magazine's beginning, and they didn't show as much as they do now. That was the beginning of an addiction to porn that would last for over 30 years.

> *Pornography is like so many other addictions: It doesn't*
> *stay where it begins, but continues to drag you*
> *farther and farther into the darkness of that world.*

Pornography is like so many other addictions: It doesn't stay where it begins, but continues to drag you farther and farther into the darkness of that world. When I was 13 or 14, I had a neighbor who worked on hot rods all the time. He had the walls and ceilings covered with pictures that had been cut out of all types of magazines. He also had stacks of magazines that hadn't had pictures removed. I spent hours every day in his shop. I now look back and realize that he enjoyed seeing a young boy look at his collection. He didn't really understand the effect it would have on me, and how many lives I would ruin over the next 20-some years.

As I got older, my addiction grew, and I became a sexual deviant.

## Hooked on Hookers

When I was 14, I had an older friend take me downtown and introduce me to prostitution. The girl standing on the corner of 12th Street and Vine in Kansas City, Missouri, sang out these words, "Five and two, five for the girl, and two for the room." Yep, seven dollars, that's what sex cost me the first time I paid for it. The very next year, 1959, Wilbert Harrison came out with a hit song called "Kansas City" in which he sings about standing on the corner of 12th Street and Vine. I started going to 12th and Central where the Folly Burlesque Theatre was and sneaking in and watching the strippers. There were doormen to keep kids out, but I soon found the fire escapes and back doors and frequented them on a regular basis.

After my experience with the prostitutes, I now had another addiction. There was something that kept drawing me back to paying a prostitute for sex, and that would continue for the next 25 years. It wasn't that I was ugly and couldn't get girls; I actually had them chasing me. There were times that I would have two or three girlfriends at the same time and be having sex with all of them, and I would still pick up hookers.

When I was in prison in the early '60s, pornography was considered contraband. You would go to the hole if you got caught with it. I had a business of selling pornography and made lots of money. Today, men in prison can actually subscribe to girlie magazines, because some studies have been done that claim pornography is not damaging. Yet I know that it is.

After my release from prison, I went into the very first adult bookstore that was opened in Kansas City. My habit continued to grow, and at times I would spend $100 a day going from one to another, all over town. I knew where every single one in Kansas City was located. Some people called them *gumshoes* because when you would walk out of those booths, your feet stuck to the floor. If you know what I'm talking about, you've probably been there.

I would go watch an hour or two of dirty movies and then go find a hooker. Then back to the bookstores and then maybe go on a date with my girlfriend. My addiction to pornography affected my relationship with every female that I came in contact with, from the prostitutes to girlfriends and of course my wives. It kept me from having the kind of intimacy with my wives that God intended between a husband and his wife. My mind was so pro-grammed from watching years and years of pornography, that by the time I got married, it was impossible to have a normal sex life. I have so many regrets today for those times and wish I could undo them. God has given me a way to make amends with those women, and I do it every time I get the chance. When I have opportunities to speak to female inmates in jails or prisons, I tell them the story of how I used to rob prostitutes and take back my money. I then ask them if they can forgive me for doing that to maybe their mothers, aunts, or just women in general. They always say that they can forgive me. By the time we are through, I am crying and they are crying, and I believe that it is healing for me and for them.

When I was about 30, I had a friend introduce me to a new way of get-ting my thrill with prostitutes. He taught me how to get my money back. This became my new sport, paying them whatever they asked and some-times a lot more, because they would treat me better. Then always – no exceptions – getting my money back. Sometimes it wasn't a pretty sight, but I never failed to get my money.

My years of using pornography led me into the swinging lifestyle, and I saw things happen in that arena that you don't ever hear about. Men that think they want to watch their wife or girlfriend with another man, and then end up losing it – breaking her jaw – then beating the other guy half to death. I am certain that people have killed their spouses because of the swinging lifestyle.

I went from soft porn to hard porn in a very short time. The progression grew to S&M, then to B&D³ movies and every sick thing that a porn produc-er could think up. When I saw my first S&M or B&D pornography movie, I thought they were perverted and never wanted to see another one. Then I actually started enjoying them and wanted to watch them and then to participate. I went so far as to watch some actual snuff movies. You have to be in the business a long time to ever see a real snuff film. I believe that if I hadn't gotten set free of pornography, I would have wanted to act out the snuff sex.

The next thing that I am going to write may sound bad, but I have rea-son to believe that if I had ever started looking at child pornography, I may have become a child molester. I can honestly say, "Thank God, I have never seen any kind of child porn." The reason I say I may have become a child molester is because every other kind of sex act I watched on film or video I acted out. The only exception was the snuff films; and as I have already stated, that is because I was delivered from pornography before that happened.

Maybe you are reading this and thinking you are not as bad as I was, but you have watched some porn and you feel it wouldn't be as bad if your wife would watch it with you. Maybe it would spice up your sex life a little bit. You've tried for months or maybe years to get her to watch one with you, and you almost have her convinced it won't hurt, but actually help your relationship. Let me tell you what's going to happen. You may be married to a woman who has never even entertained the idea of cheating on you. She doesn't look at other men and think about sleeping with them. When you watch a porn flick with that kind of woman, for the first time in her life, as she watches the reaction of the girl in the movie, she is going to wonder what it would be like to be with another man. Is that what you want to bring into your marriage? NO! It is not. I have seen marriages destroyed by bringing pornography into them.

Do you remember in this article when I referred to porn movies as *dirty movies*? Did you ever wonder, *Why are they called dirty movies? Why are they called dirty jokes? Who gave them that name?* Usually the guy telling it, he walks up and says, "Do you want to hear a dirty joke?" Think about that for a minute, even the guy telling it calls it dirty. Why would we want something dirty to enter our mind?

> **I have seen marriages destroyed by bringing pornography into them.**

Maybe you are just starting to look at soft porn, or maybe you are already addicted beyond what you think is a place of no return. Take it from someone who has been as deep into the world of pornography as you can get. I was so deep in the darkness of that world that the only thing I could do to get out was to do a completely radical 180-degree turn. I began my journey of getting out of that world by asking Jesus Christ to come into my heart and take over my life. There is a saying in the computer world. "Trash in . . . trash out." A friend of mine told me, if I filled my head full of good things, it would drive the trash out. So he told me if I wanted to read a magazine, read a Christian magazine. If I wanted to listen to the radio, listen to Christian radio. If I wanted to watch TV, watch Christian TV. If I wanted to talk to someone, talk to a Christian. You get the picture, Christian, Christian,

Christian. This may not be what everyone has to do, but it was the only thing I could do. If you are as addicted to porn as I was, it may be the only thing you *can* do. I promise you it will work, if you do it seriously. It is like anything else: If you only half do it, it only half works. If you go to the gym every day and watch people work out, you are not going to get in shape. The only way it will work is if you go work out.

# THE ULTIMATE PARDON

When you realize that you can't fix your life and you need to give your life over to God, this is what the Bible calls "salvation," "getting saved," or being "born again[1]."

> *I filled my head  so full of the truth that I pushed all the lies out.*

You may need to find someone to confess to and ask them to be your accountability partner. After meeting with my accountability partner, I spent hours in the Bible every day. I filled my head so full of the truth that I pushed all the lies out. I hope this book helps you, and I really hope my little assistance helped you as well. Bless you, and may the Lord make His face to shine upon you.

In HIS grip,
Bill Corum
II Corinthians 5:17
*www.theultimatepardon.com*
*www.billcorum.com*
www.youtube.com/Bill CorumTestimony

You can read in detail more of Bill's experiences in his autobiography, *The Ultimate Pardon.*

---

1 For further discussion on what it means to "be saved", refer to What Does it Mean to "Get Saved"? in the appendix, on page 211.

**Reflections:**

1. Would you be willing to take the test to see if you are addicted?

   Yes_____ No_____   Take an online test at:

   *http://www.pornaddictioninfo.com/addict_quiz.htm*
   *http://www.sexhelp.com/am-i-a-sex-addict/sex-addiction-test*

2. On a scale of 1 – 10 how addicted are you?  Number 1 is "Porn is not an issue for me" and 10 is "I am an addict". Rate what you found:

$$1 - 2 - 3 - 4 - 5 - 6 - 7 - 8 - 9 - 10$$

3. If Bill was "as deep into the world of pornography as you can get" and Jesus was able to help him, is there hope for you?
   Yes_____ No_____

4. What is the first step you need to take to begin this journey?

   _____
   _____
   _____
   _____
   _____
   _____
   _____

# YOU SAW *WHO* AT THE STRIP CLUB?

Tom[2] had attended our men's groups off and on for about three years. When he first came, he couldn't even talk in the small check-in groups, let alone speak up in the large-group time.

He had struggled with sexual addiction for many years. He was finally beginning to make some progress and attend group regularly when he had a huge crash. One night when he was very discouraged, he went back to something he had done many years earlier: He went to a strip club.

Tom found the clubs to be even more intoxicating than in the past. He purchased many lap dances and experienced the physical touch and counterfeit joy of conversations with young women who were attractive and "friendly" to him.

> *While powerfully intoxicating in the moment, these experiences left him in great pain and filled with deep shame.*

While powerfully intoxicating in the moment, these experiences left him in great pain and filled with deep shame. In his shame, he found himself returning to the club occasionally and at one point having thoughts of suicide. He had also started meeting regularly with me for a counseling process called the Immanuel Process.

Immanuel Prayer[4] comes from Jesus' promise in Matthew 28:20, "I am with you always to the very end of the age." In its most basic form, Immanuel Prayer is simply asking Jesus to show us where He was during certain painful experiences. Many times individuals will get words or images in their memories. It helps them see that Jesus was really with them during this horrible time.

Tom had found a very sweet place with Jesus in our previous session

---

2   Not his real name.

so I encouraged him to remember it. Next, I told him to ask Jesus where He wanted him to go today. I saw him physically tense up as he said, "I am getting an image from the strip club." My first thought was that Satan was trying to distract him or bring shame, so I prayed and then had him ask Jesus again where He wanted him to go.

His response was, "I'm still in the strip club with the young woman who was nice to me." While I was somewhat surprised, I hesitantly asked, "Do you see Jesus anywhere?"

Immediately Tom perked up a little and said in a surprised tone, "Yeah, He is right there, just above her."

"Is He upset or angry with you?" I asked.

"No, He seems sad, but still glad to be with me." The only thing I could think of was to have him ask Jesus questions. I instructed him to ask if there was anything Jesus wanted to say to him. Immediately a tear trickled down Tom's face as he replied: "Jesus said, 'I know you are here because your pain is great. However, what you need is not her, but Me.'"

> *Jesus said, 'I know you are here because your pain is great. However, what you need is not her, but Me.*

Tom felt, heard, and understood. He knew Jesus saw his sin and his pain but did not condemn him; instead He offered the solution for his sin. The solution, of course, was learning that Tom's deepest need was not for sex or even the touch or delight of a woman, but simply Jesus himself.

That was about a year ago, and Tom has not been back to a strip club. He has had only one momentary slip in his recovery since Jesus met him there. He continues to find Jesus in new places, and his continued change is evident to everyone who knows him.

Every time I meet with him, I see new strength, confidence, and growth. He now speaks freely in our small groups, and what he shares in the big-group time has become an encouragement to many. It is important to note that he has also been faithful in other recovery behaviors. He works on materials, calls men from the groups, and attends multiple meetings every week.

Darrell Brazell [5]
www.NewHope4si.com
*http://newhopelawrence.com*

**Reflections:**

1. Does it feel true to you that your deepest needs are not your sexual desires or even sex with a woman, but your deepest need is to have a relationship with Jesus Himself? Explain why or why not. _____

_____

_____

_____

_____

2. It might seem strange that Jesus went to a strip club, but the Bible tells stories of Jesus hanging out with the undesirables – the prostitutes, tax collectors, the lepers, the outcasts, etc. If Jesus was physically on earth today where do you think he would hang out? _____

_____

_____

_____

_____

3. Would he come to a jail cell or to where you live or workplace to help you? _____

_____

_____

_____

Write a simple invitation asking Him to come where you are now.

_____

_____

_____

_____

_____

_____

# PORNOGRAPHY—THE ULTIMATE BAIT AND SWITCH

Why is porn so difficult for men to walk away from?   Porn is a perfect example of bait-and-switch.

A bait-and-switch concept is something that is based on a false claim. The claim ends up being a disappointment. This is a perfect definition of porn.

Joy is what we really desire and pornography is a pseudo or counterfeit joy, used to distract us from what we really want and need.

> *If you struggle with porn, you aren't alone. Each second 28,258 Internet users are viewing pornography. Over $3000 is spent on porn every second, and 97 billion dollars a year around the globe.[6] There are 4.2 million pornographic websites, 420 million pornographic web pages, and 68 million daily search engine requests.[7]*

## The Bait

Anticipation. Just sitting at the computer gets you going. As you move from one page to another you feel the rush. Your heart races as you scan the faces of the models and actresses reflecting their insatiable longings and the invitation for you to be with them. Your breathing gets shallow as you search through images looking for one that will satisfy you. This visually induced dopamine rush gives you a high like no other as you choose the beauty you want, beauty with absolutely no strings attached.

In your fantasy world, you can live through the actresses on the screen, or you can control what happens in your imagination -- how you perform, and how the immensely attractive young woman responds to you. This woman can read your mind, saying what you want to hear, and doing what you ask, again and again and again. It seems like the ultimate experience because you alone are in total control of what happens.

And these websites, full of the hottest young porn stars, seem unlimited. They are available for your pleasure 24/7. Who could want more?

But then you open your eyes and you're alone. Reality crashes in -- those hot young models aren't there with you. You'll never meet them and even if you did, they wouldn't want you anyway. It's just you and a screen you can't resist watching.

There wasn't a real woman to cuddle with you and whisper in your ear that she loves you and always will. You're just alone, alone and addicted to a glowing, electronic box. . .

### The Switch

What is the result of all this exposure to pornographic pictures and videos? Stop and ponder this question. Is it nothing?    How am I affected? Who is strengthened?   Who is hurt? Although there are many risks and drawbacks to using porn, we'll examine just three: 1) Addiction, 2) Lack of intimacy in relationship and 3) loss of ability to perform sexually with a real woman.

### Addiction

The sex industry comes after men, marketing to them, baiting them. The lure of the air- brushed photos or the unrealistic video is the bait. And of course our society tells us it's cool and attractive, encouraging us to chase after women in the promise of finally achieving the ultimate sexual experience and the ultimate orgasm. Unfortunately, the porn consumer, in a short time, becomes a porn addict.

> *"Do not bite at the bait of pleasure till you know there is no hook beneath it." Thomas Jefferson*

Then comes the sad reality. The lack of intimacy, the shame, going down darker and darker pathways pursuing fix after fix, just to get the same thrill. Porn takes men into darker and riskier places, often going from porn to personal encounters. Now you're on the road to addiction and you can't get out.

> ***Did you know that the brain scans for men who use porn regularly look exactly like the brain scan of a drug addict?***

When used addictively, sex becomes like a drug. Scientists have actually discovered that brain scans of porn addicts look like those of drug addicts.[3] You simply can't get enough of what won't satisfy you. If you keep trying to get that "something" – whatever it is that you get over and over again, while remaining unsatisfied – you're an addict.[8]

Sex becomes an addiction when need and compulsion drive sexual behaviors. Sex is no longer about sharing joy with your wife, but it's about getting a fix and an orgasm on demand. Because porn triggers the release of Dopamine and other feel-good chemicals the momentary pleasure is high, but the hunger returns as quickly as the shame. The shame itself triggers more hunger and the destructive spiral accelerates.

This destructive spiral affects our relationships as well.

> ***One in five people who regularly watch porn admitted to feeling controlled by their sexual desires…. .***[9]

### Lack of Intimacy in Relationships

Porn causes men to view women as objects for their own personal pleasure. Porn presents women in stereotype, as sexual beings who are here to please men, and if they say *no* they don't really mean it. In pornography, the typical woman is always ready, available, and eager to please, unlike any real woman, (or the porn star when the cameras aren't rolling.) Women have no value or meaning, and their desires and needs are irrelevant. The image of sexuality offered by pornography comes without relationships, responsibility or consequences. Pornography is not about a real, satisfying human relationship: it's about a version of sex that eliminates love, honor, respect, dignity, true intimacy and commitment. Porn paints a false picture of relationships in every way possible.

Eighty-two percent of those who claim sexual satisfaction say they feel respected by their partner.[10] Pornography slowly destroys a man's ability to appreciate and love a woman purely for herself. It teaches that the main

---

3 *http://www.gq.com/blogs/the-feed/2013/11/10-reasons-why-you-should-quit-watching-porn.html*

function of what *should be a sensitive and satisfying relationship between two people* is merely self-gratification.

Sexual activity is not intended to be only about sexual release, but about joy and intimacy with one special person. Intimacy includes all the elements of our lives -- the physical, the social, emotional, mental and spiritual. Together, these are the pathways to share your whole life, and to experience the closeness that sex inside a committed relationship will bring. Porn makes this mutual respect impossible leading to failed relationships.

> ### Men were created for so much more than just the physical.

Men were created for so much more than just the physical. God created men to be protectors and lovers of the women with whom they share their marriage bed and their lives. They were created for intimate joy with their wives in a committed marriage relationship. Men can receive the joy and delight they long for when they love their wife in and out of the bedroom. This is actually what both marital partners deeply desire and deserve.

> ### Married couples have more frequent and more satisfying sex than porn users.[11]

Married couples have more frequent and more satisfying sex than porn users.[11] If you want good sex get emotionally healthy and be faithful and kind to one woman, in a totally committed marital relationship. It's the opposite of what porn tells you! If you think using porn will give you more intimacy and more satisfying sex you're wrong. It doesn't. Porn is a bait-and-switch.

### Loss of Ability to Perform Sexually With A Real Woman

Men who view porn not only acquire wrong information about women and relationships, they also pick up false expectations which spoil their sexual enjoyment, causing them to doubt their own adequacy. They become overly concerned about their sexual performance and how their bodies look. They become less satisfied with their spouse's body. Porn trains men to be unhappy with their spouse, unhappy with their own body, and to doubt their adequacy.

Porn also trains its viewers to expect constant newness. Viewing one seductive young airbrushed woman after another on the internet leads to the need for larger doses of different, strange situations and strange bodies to maintain arousal, and it often makes it difficult to maintain arousal with one real woman. The more pornography a man watches, the more likely he is to need to think of pornographic images during sex to maintain his arousal. He is also more likely to ask his partner to act out particular pornographic sex acts. The higher the use of pornography, the less enjoyment there is during sex with a partner.[12]

Also, an even more common problem for porn-using men is the problem of premature ejaculation. A man who uses pornography and masturbation trains his brain and his body to achieve climax quickly which is not how the female body operates sexually.[13] God gave the gift of sexual intimacy as a way for a husband and wife to share a powerful joy connection.

God gave us sex and it is like a bonding tool in our brains and that by viewing and masturbating to porn men (or women) bond themselves to images and sexual situations. These images supplant real relationship bonding (i.e. attachment). We therefore, lose our God-given ability to feel a joyful connection with our spouse because self-sex is bonding us with pornographic images. Porn has rerouted our brain's connections and our memories of porn now become the center of attachment and we don't connect with wives.[14]

### Hummingbirds and Sustained Nourishment

If you fill a hummingbird feeder with sugar water and the birds get accustomed to feeding from it, and then switch the sugar water to artificially sweetened water, the hummingbirds will die. Artificial sweeteners aren't poisonous to hummingbirds but the birds die of starvation. What seems like food to them has no calories for their bodies to use as fuel.

> *Hallah from New York states, "I believe two people in love is sexy. Not one person and their computer screen."*[15]

This is a great analogy for pornography and sexual addiction. God created us with an innate hunger and need for joyful, relational connections. We all long for and need to be with people who are genuinely "glad as glad can be to be with me." At first pornography seems to provide that connection; after all, what speaks this message more clearly to a man (or a young boy for that matter) than a beautiful woman dressed in a provocative manner as the object his delight? It is close, but it is a bait-and-switch. It provides excitement, pleasure and chemical activity in the brain. It becomes candy: lots of calories, but no nutrition. It feels good temporarily but has no sustaining power, slowly starving all other intimate relationships.[16]

**Reflections:**

1. "Pornography is a self-centered activity, something a man does by himself, for himself -- by using women as the means to pleasure, or a product to consume." Do you agree? Why or why not? _____

   _____

   _____

   _____

   _____

2. "God created men to be protectors and lovers of the women with whom they share their marriage bed and their lives." Which are you, a consumer or protector? _____

   If you are a consumer, write down one thing you can do to change this. If you are a protector, how can you improve? _____

   _____

   _____

3. What are the promises that porn makes? _____

   _____

   _____

   _____

   _____

   _____

   What are true results of porn use?_____

   _____

   _____

   _____

   _____

   _____

   _____

   _____

# THE BRAIN ON PORN

A path through the woods becomes larger with each new hiker. It's the same thing with the brain. As men fall deep into the mental habit of viewing pornography neural pathways are forming in the brain. Each time you look at an erotic image these neural paths are triggered. They become the automatic pathways through which all contact with women are directed. Those who repeatedly view porn have unknowingly created a circuit in the brain which keeps them from viewing women appropriately. Their brains are actually rewired into an addictive habit.

Scientists at Cambridge University recently studied the brain scans of porn addicts and found that they looked remarkably similar exactly like those of drug addicts.[17] Sex, cocaine, and many other drugs all stimulate the same pleasure center of the brain where dopamine is released. Dopamine is a neurotransmitter that helps control the brain's reward and pleasure centers. People with low dopamine levels may be more prone to addictions.[18]

Because of the way that the brain functions, it's impossible to keep getting the same "high" off of drugs or porn without continuing to increase the dosage.

Just like other addictive substances, porn floods the brain with dopamine. But since the brain gets overwhelmed by the constant overload of chemicals that comes with consistent porn use, it fights back by taking away some of its dopamine receptors....

With fewer receptors, even if the brain is putting off the same levels of dopamine in response to porn, the user can't feel dopamine's effect as much. As a result, the porn they were looking at doesn't seem as arousing or exciting, and most porn users go hunting for more porn or more hardcore porn, or progress beyond porn to more stimulating and damaging forms of acting out to get the effect the old porn used to offer.

As a frequent porn user's brain acclimates to the new levels of dopamine flooding through it, regular activities that would normally set off a burst of dopamine and make the person feel happy aren't strong enough to register much anymore, leaving the user feeling down or uneasy whenever they go for a while without looking at porn. That's one reason why pornography can be so addictive.

Once addiction sets in, the user has a whole new set of problems, because addiction damages the part of the brain that helps you think things through to make good choices....[19] And here's the really scary part: the more porn a person looks at, the more severe the damage to their brain becomes and the more difficult it is to break free. But there's good news too.... the damage to the brain can be undone when someone gets away from unhealthy behaviors.[20]

In most ways sexual addiction is just like other addictions. However, the shame and social taboos associated with it often make it an even more difficult and baffling enemy. The good news, however, is that there is hope. We have seen many individuals face their addiction head-on in community and find freedom and healing[21]."

**Reflections:**

1.  What started your porn use? Circle all that apply:  Hooked as a child, lack of intimacy, vulnerability, low self-esteem, rejection, pain from past experiences, Dad's example. Anything else?_____

    _____
    _____
    _____
    _____
    _____

2.  What keeps you coming back to porn? _____

    _____
    _____
    _____
    _____
    _____

3.  Describe the process in the brain that makes a porn user need to keep seeing more graphic porn in order to get the same rush._____

    _____
    _____
    _____
    _____
    _____
    _____
    _____

# A LITTLE HELP FROM MY FRIENDS

We all need a little help from our friends. But if we're addicted, we need a lot of help from our friends, counselors, and group members.

The healing of sexual addictions comes, in part, by establishing healthy relationships. Recovery isn't only about gaining information, or how to overcome addictions, it's also about building relationships with people who are genuinely glad to be with you.

That's why Alcoholics Anonymous (or other recovery meetings such as Celebrate Recovery) is effective. They meet as a group and have partners. These prove the power of close-knit relationships to help battle an addiction. . . . .

> *Social isolation is as potent a cause of early death as smoking cigarettes a day and loneliness is twice as deadly as obesity.*[22]

The importance of emotional support is proven by several fascinating scientific studies. The first study about rats was taken from an article entitled *The Likely Cause of Addiction Has Been Discovered, and It Is Not What You Think* by Johann Hari.[23]

Scientists put a rat in a cage, alone, with two water bottles. One has just water. The other is water laced with heroin or cocaine. Almost every time you run this experiment, the rat will become obsessed with the drugged water, and keep coming back for more and more, until it kills itself.....

But in the 1970s, a professor of Psychology in Vancouver called Bruce Alexander noticed something odd about this experiment. The rat is put in the cage all alone. It has nothing to do but take the drugs. What would happen, he wondered, if we tried this differently? So Professor Alexander built Rat Park. It is a lush cage where the rats would have colored balls and the best rat-food and tunnels to scamper down and plenty of friends: everything a rat about town could want. What, Alexander wanted to know, will happen then?

In Rat Park, all the rats obviously tried both water bottles, because they didn't know what was in them. But what happened next was startling.

The rats with good lives, within community, didn't like the drugged water. They mostly shunned it, consuming less than a quarter of the drugs the isolated rats used. None of them died. While all the rats who were alone and unhappy became heavy drug users, none of the rats who had a happy environment did.

After the first phase of Rat Park, Professor Alexander then took this test further. He reran the early experiments, where the rats were left alone, and became compulsive users of the drug. He let them use for fifty-seven days[4] — if anything can hook you, it's that. Then he took them out of isolation, and placed them in Rat Park. He wanted to know, if you fall into that state of addiction, is your brain hijacked, so you can't recover? Do the drugs take you over? What happened is — again — striking. The rats seemed to have a few twitches of withdrawal, but they soon stopped their heavy use, and went back to having a normal life. The good cage, with community life, saved them.

Professor Peter Cohen argues that human beings have a deep need to bond and form connections. It's how we get our satisfaction. If we can't connect with each other, we will connect with anything we can find.... So the opposite of addiction is not always sobriety. It is human connection. This is the power of staying busy and being with people who can help you.

A man who isolates himself seeks his own desire; He rages against all wise judgment. Proverbs 18:1

> ***So the opposite of addiction is not always sobriety.***
> ***It is human connection.***

Equally fascinating is a research project in Virginia that asked students (wearing a weighted backpack) to describe the steepness of a hill. Some stood and looked at the hill alone and some stood with friends. The students who stood with a friend said the hill didn't look as steep as it did to those who were alone.[25]

This is a great visual picture as you stand wearing a weighted backpack called addiction facing a steep hill to climb called recovery. The right friends

---

4   When you realize that the average lifespan of a rat is only a few years, then this becomes even more significant.

can help you conquer what you believe you cannot conquer alone simply because they are standing with you. Keep reading and you'll see that there is hope for you to kick the porn habit and find the kind of satisfaction you're looking for, in a real relationship.

**Reflections:**

1. How would you explain to a friend why the rats in Rat Park were able to overcome their addictions? _____

   _____

   _____

   _____

   _____

2. Do you have a friend or acquaintance who understands you and is not a porn user? Write down a time to talk with him and ask for help. Date and location _____

   Let him know how much this means to you. Write down what you will tell him. _____

   _____

   _____

   _____

3. If you don't have a friend or acquaintance, don't give up. Support groups are also effective. Write down the name of a group you can join and the time and place that they meet. _____

   _____

   _____

   Many are free. Will you commit to attending the next meeting?

   _____

4. Make an appointment with a therapist skilled in helping people through addictions. Write down your appointment time:

   _____

Following through on any one of these could be one of the most significant and important turning points in your life!

# THE VICTIMS OF PORN

Porn users like to say: "Well I am not hurting anyone." Yet there are very real victims: wives, children and the women who are exploited by porn.

### Partners and Wives

When women in a committed relationship learn that their partner has been using porn they often report feeling loss, betrayal, mistrust, devastation, and anger.[26] Many women show physical symptoms of anxiety and depression. Some show signs of PTSD, and some even become suicidal.[27] For many women, their partner's porn use made them feel like the entire relationship was a complete deception.[28]

The more pornography a man watches, the more likely he is to ask his partner to act out pornographic sexual acts.[29] Women report that they are asked to act or do things they're uncomfortable with or find demeaning.[30]

The following quotes are taken from a woman whose husband was addicted to pornography. His behavior finally led to a divorce. This is how she explained it:

- "I was feeling like I was a prostitute in my bed."
- "It was like he was masturbating in my own body."
- "You feel like you are just a body to him. I did not feel like his wife or his 'beloved'"
- "It hurt me deeply when I knew my husband got his sexual pleasure from looking at other women."
- "I was often asked to do something that did not seem safe, comfortable, or loving."

The average woman knows she can't compete with the surgically enhanced, air-brushed, and Photoshopped porn star. Six out of seven women feel that porn has raised men's expectations of how women should look.[31]

Women feel like they can't measure up. One wife felt like her husband preferred even the image, over her. "It really sank me."

Porn harms marriages and families. At the 2003 meeting of the American Academy of Matrimonial Lawyers, a gathering of the nation's divorce lawyers, attendees revealed that 58% of their divorces were a result of a spouse looking at excessive amounts of pornography online.[32]

> *"I believe that cocaine, heroin, and methamphetamine have nothing on pornography when it comes to destroying families and destroying lives," Ken Wallentine, chief of law enforcement with the Utah attorney general's office.*[33]

### Porn Models and Actresses

Also victimized, but hidden from sight, is the woman branded as an enthusiastic model in the porn film. Men who use porn don't see what happens *after* the camera stops: the sensual model who was "enjoying it" often ends up curled up in a ball of pain or later being treated for an STD. Pornography is sexual fantasy turned destructive. One former porn star said that drugs and alcohol are common on the sets because no woman could film those scenes sober.

The average life span of a porn star is 36 years.[34] The average life expectancy for men and women in the United States is 77 years.[35] What's going on? Is this really a glamorous, desirable profession that has no victims?

### Children

For every man who consumes child porn there is a young victim. Child pornography is one of the fastest growing businesses online, and the content is becoming much worse.

While not all men who use porn will advance to child porn and child abuse, almost no one who abuses children isn't involved with porn and child porn. It's unusual for prosecutors to find child sex abuse that didn't begin with or involve child pornography. "Every time we find a child predator, almost without fail, you can track back and find that pornography and child pornography was part of the picture.... The links are frightening and they are powerful."[36]

> Samuel Seager was sentenced in 2008 to as many as 75 years in prison for the child abuse that lasted close to four

years. One thing he does know is that the abuse and pornography worked hand-in-hand. What he saw — which, at first was so repulsive to him — became less and less so as time went on. Pornography changed the way he treated his victim.[37]

---

*When you read enough pornography, over a period of time, it gets ingrained. What was once disgusting becomes arousing. There have been many times that I've cursed the day I first saw those 3 or 4 porno magazines. (Anonymous)*

---

"It's safe to say that the abuse was more aggressive, pronounced or worse because of (pornography)...." Seager said he'd never touched child pornography until an accidental search of the history on a friend's computer.... "I saw some terrible, terrible things out there and as I kept searching, those things weren't so terrible anymore...."

A religious man, he said he would pray every single night for the power to stop. But he, in turn, would spend his days nourishing his urges. "I wouldn't let it go," he said. "I was constantly seeking it out. I was always trying to feed it."

"I kept thinking about it. I kept wanting it and so, of course, I'm not going to let it go," he said. "What I realized once I got here (behind bars) was, 'Wow, I was holding on so tight to that thing.'

A study of 341 convicted, American child molesters, found that using pornography was significantly related to their rate of sexually re-offending. High risk offenders viewed porn more frequently and the more deviant the porn, the higher the chances that they would molest again.[38]

---

*"I saw some terrible, terrible things out there and as I kept searching, those things weren't so terrible anymore."*

---

Here is an eye-opening statistic from an organization called *Enough is Enough*. Unfortunately, behind every statistic there are children who are who, apart from God, are emotionally handicapped for life.

- The number of Internet child pornography images has increased

1500% since 1988. Approximately 20% of all Internet pornography involves children.[39]

Commercial child pornography is a $20 billion industry fueled by the Internet[40] and it creates victims worldwide. Cyberspace has provided an advantage to pornography sellers, including those harming children. People can link to the website from anywhere in the world in real time, and for money they can request sexual acts and watch them being performed on children! This is what is to come as the world connects itself and its addictions to sex online.

Most of these victimized children are from impoverished families in developing countries. . . Orphans are among the most sought out.[41]

One therapist writes: "When a child experiences reality beyond their readiness, they have no means of processing the material intellectually or emotionally. At that time, they will bury the experience in their unconscious, where it will lurk in the shadows haunting them, possibly for the rest of their lives."[42] [43]

*Enough Is Enough* former President Dee Jepsen states:

> Some say pornography doesn't have any victims. I know better. I look into the tear-filled eyes of victims nearly every time I speak.... Women spoke of husbands who insisted they imitate scenes from pornography, whether they wished to or not. Doctors spoke of sexual dysfunction and unrealistic expectations due to pornography. Law enforcement officials spoke of pornography's connection to sexual crimes. And men spoke of the damage they had witnessed, or caused, because of pornography use.

> Offer yourselves to sin, for instance, and it's your last free act. But offer yourselves to the ways of God and the freedom never quits. All your lives you've let sin tell you what to do. But thank God you've started listening to a new master, one whose commands set you free to live openly in *his* freedom! *Romans 6:16-18* The Message Bible

**Reflections:**

1. Take a moment to consider how this addiction has affected your close
personal relationships with women and/or children. What can you do to
improve these relationships? _____

_____

_____

_____

_____

2. Samuel Seager said that he "would spend my days nourishing my urges.
I wouldn't let it go...I was constantly seeking it out. I was always trying to feed it." Is it surprising that he eventually acted out what he was
thinking? _____

How could he have prevented this? _____

_____

_____

_____

_____

3. If you have been involved with child porn are you ready to acknowledge
that and leave it behind? If yes then write your thoughts down here: ___

_____

_____

_____

_____

_____

Now say these thoughts as a prayer to God and listen for His reply. Write
what He said:_____

_____

_____

_____

_____

_____

_____

_____

**Here is a helpful scripture in a more modern version of the Bible, called The Message Bible. Memorize it and quote it frequently:**

**James 4:7-10** So let God work His will in you. Yell a loud *no* to the Devil and watch him scamper. Say a quiet *yes* to God and He'll be there in no time. Quit dabbling in sin. Purify your inner life. Quit playing the field. Hit bottom, and cry your eyes out. The fun and games are over. Get serious, really serious. *Get down on your knees before the Master; it's the only way you'll get on your feet.*

# BREAKING POINT

Pastor Darrell Brazell writes an honest, poignant story of his multi-year battle against masturbation and porn and their negative effects on his marriage and ministry. Darrell addresses the core issues spiritually, behaviorally, and psychologically that are at the foundation of sexual bondage and addiction. He describes the grueling process of confession, accountability, and eventual victory and the lessons he learned along the way. This article was originally published in *Christianity Today* magazine.

### One pastor's story of pain, porn, addiction, and redemption

It's 1:45 p.m. on Tuesday, and I'm logging on to the Internet to check my e-mail, read a newspaper article, and begin research for Sunday's sermon.

Well, that's what I'm trying to convince myself of.

But I know exactly what I'm doing. When my secretary leaves at 2:00, I will be alone in the building. I will check my e-mail, and I may read an article or two. But as soon as the door closes behind her, I will do what I have done more times than I care to count: I'll type "sex" or "porn" or something worse in the search engine and spend the next three or four hours in the pigpen.

I will enter a trance that leads me to neglect important projects, ignore phone calls, and lose track of time. Eventually I will look at the clock and panic because my wife was expecting me home 15 minutes ago, and I have just started trashing files, clearing the search history, and doing what I can to put myself back together. I'll use every minute of my drive home to create an excuse for being late. I'll try to put on a good face even though I know pornography makes real connection impossible. Usually I fail miserably and end up in a fight with my wife in my first 30 minutes at home.

On Wednesday, I'll go to the office committed to not answer the siren call of the porn sites. I'll start the morning in prayer, confessing my sin and begging God to give me a fresh start. I'll return the phone calls I ignored on Tuesday and work diligently on my midweek lesson. I'll do fine all morning, but when the secretary leaves, the battle will rage again. Most Wednesdays I'll win, though I'll still feel the shame of Tuesday when I stand before my evening Bible class.

Thursday is usually a nightmare; Friday is repentance day. Time and again Friday begins with tearful prayers, begging for God's mercy and promising next week will be different. I then scramble to write my sermon. Sunday mornings I arrive at the building early so I can beg God for a fresh start and finish my sermon. Standing in the pulpit Sunday after Sunday, I constantly hear the inner condemnation: Who are you to proclaim God's holy Word? And What would they think if they knew? One Sunday, the enemy pounded me throughout the worship service so intensely that during the song before communion, I seriously contemplated not partaking. The hypocrisy was so apparent to me that I seriously considered not taking communion. Imagine what it would look like if the pastor in the second row refused the elements?

Thankfully, what I've described is now 12 years behind me. Its roots, however, go all the way back to my early childhood. I've heard alcoholics say they were addicted from the very first drink. I understand that feeling. When I was introduced to pornography at about age 10, it was like throwing gasoline on a fire. The dysfunctions and neglect in my family left me hurting and looking for ways to numb the pain. I learned very quickly that sex is a powerful drug.

## The Anatomy of Addiction

At first, I shared magazines with friends, caught R-rated movies on cable, and occasionally acquired harder materials. My struggle escalated my senior year in high school when I realized I looked old enough to purchase porn. That's when I developed a binge-purge cycle. I would buy a magazine, use it once or twice, and then (the first time I was home alone) take it to our burning barrel and set it ablaze in a ritual of repentance.

The epitome of this cycle was the day I lit a magazine on fire and dropped it into the empty barrel. As it fell, the flame went out. I stared down into the barrel knowing I couldn't just leave it there. I finally changed into an old shirt, climbed halfway into the barrel and retrieved it so I could light it again. Unfortunately, in the time it took me to rescue the magazine, my conviction faded, and instead of burning the magazine, I devoured it some more.

This binge-purge cycle led to an incredible sense of guilt and shame. I wanted to tell somebody, but the horror of sharing my shame kept me silent. The whole time, I honestly loved God and begged him to take away my struggle. But I couldn't find freedom.

Graduation posed an important decision. I had felt a call to ministry since junior high. Some days I felt that my struggle with sexual addiction disqualified me from ministry. Other times I felt that if I made the commitment to pursue God's plan for my life, He would take the struggle away. Ultimately I went to Bible College to become a pastor. My addiction didn't disappear at school, but it did change shape. I rarely gave in to pornography, but masturbation became so ritualistic I couldn't go to sleep at night without it. The cycle was the same: guilt, shame, and repentance culminating with a promise to God to never do it again.

My junior year, I talked an incredible young woman into marrying me. I naively thought getting married and having marital sex would solve the problem. It actually made the problem worse, as the fear of being found out by the one I loved most drove me to deeper levels of hiding. Sex was good, but it was never good enough, because I was never really there.

I kept the problem at a maintenance level for many years, only acting out with pornography when my wife was out of town. Even then, I didn't view what most would consider "porn," but R-rated movies with sexual themes or content. However, when I got my first laptop with Internet access, the problem exploded. Suddenly I didn't have to risk someone recognizing me. I could download anything I wanted in the safety and anonymity of my home or office.

Twice I confessed my struggle to my wife. Both times it hurt her greatly, but she forgave me and believed my promise to change. But my resolve was always short-lived.

I wanted desperately to share my struggle with someone else. But with whom? By now, I was a solo pastor. If I confessed to one of my elders or congregants, I could lose my job. More importantly, I was supposed to be the spiritual guide for my community of faith. What does it say when the "spiritual guide" is consumed by sin and shame?

On two occasions I mustered the courage to confess my struggle to a fellow pastor. One of them said, "You know it's wrong, so don't do it anymore." The other said, "I'm in it deeper than you. All we can do is depend on God to work in spite of our sin." Neither answer offered much hope.

We moved to a different church. It was harder than I anticipated. We left a grace-oriented church for one that was struggling and had little understanding of real grace. External appearances were especially important there, so my wife and I both felt immense pressure to smile and project the "everything is wonderful" persona.

This heightened my insecurity. Worse yet, my marriage was in trouble. I had distanced myself so much from my wife and daughter that they chose to make life good without me. The way we ate our meals illustrated my isolation. We often sat at the breakfast bar with my daughter on one end, me on the other, and my wife in between, feeding our child with her back to me.

Despite all this, I felt I was gaining control of my struggle. I had vowed to go a year without viewing pornography. I figured that once I had a year behind me, I could safely speak of my addiction in the past tense and everything would be fine.

So I white-knuckled it. However, one way I controlled it was by using masturbation as my drug. If my wife and I did not have sex, I simply took care of myself.

A few months after the move, my wife went out of town, and I binged again. I was devastated beyond description. I contemplated suicide. I wondered if this was the end of my marriage and my ministry. I wanted desperately to tell someone. I felt ashamed, worthless, and trapped.

For two months I fought for the courage to tell my wife. I needed her to change the password on the Internet filter, or I would return to the pigpen as soon as I was home alone. But I honestly feared that this time she would leave and not come back. By the grace of God, however, I told her and she didn't leave, but we knew we had to find an answer.

The next week, I went to a pastors' retreat where a man shared his struggle with pornography and described how he found freedom. I also picked up the book *Pure Desire*. Together with the testimony of someone who had found a way out, this book was the beginning of my recovery.

But I was still alone. After the retreat I began asking God to send someone to walk the journey with me, someone in whom I could safely confide, someone who was also determined to find victory.

Shortly thereafter, God sent a young man who confessed his struggle with pornography to me. I'm quite certain he received the last thing he expected when I replied, "I guess you are the one for whom I've been praying." He looked at me in shock. I then told him my story and about the resources I had found. That morning we agreed to meet weekly, talk on the phone, and work through materials together.

What followed was the most painful year of my life. Many nights I was still awake at 3 a.m., sitting on the bottom step to our basement sobbing and asking God when the pain would subside. Most of the time I didn't have a clue what hurt; I just knew it was excruciating. My mind kept screaming to go online, turn on the TV, do something—anything—to numb it. But I learned that whenever I stood in the pain long enough, I always discovered God was enough. Meeting with Him was worth the struggle.

My marriage continued to suffer. I wasn't looking at pornography or engaging in solo sex, but in my addicted core, I still believed the lie that sex was like oxygen and that I could not survive without it. As a result, I put incredible pressure on my wife. The nights we didn't have sex, especially the nights we fought, often sent me to the steps crying out to God.

I danced on the edge many times, yet somehow, by God's grace, I refused to give in to the powerful pull. Even if it meant not sleeping all night, I refused to give in. God always found a way to see me through the battle. Day by day He taught me that He could get me through anything, that I was not defined by my sin but by my Savior. He revealed His delight in me even when I was a sobbing mess on my bottom step. He comforted me and showed me His truth countering the lie that sex was like oxygen. He showed me that what I really needed wasn't pornography, a sexual release, or even my wife's body, but Him.

Because my primary confidant during this first year was a young single man in my church, I held many things back. I experienced moments of grace through him when I shared what I could. But I too often allowed my role as his pastor to give me an excuse to not be fully transparent. Fortunately God began bringing other men into my life and giving me the courage to share more completely with them.

Eventually I told my story to a pastor in my community. He offered another glimpse of grace and a second point of accountability. A few months later, I told my story to a half dozen pastors at a luncheon. I found that every time I shared my real struggle with others, I grew stronger and more able to resist temptation.

I became a student of sexual addiction. I read everything I could find, both secular and Christian. These books put words to my feelings and helped me make sense of myself. Much of what they described went beyond my experience, but I identified with the people in their books nonetheless. I began to glean from them specific strategies for walking away from my addictive behaviors. Every book insisted that it is crucial to share this struggle with others, which confirmed my need for the community of men God was establishing around me.

Later in my journey, John Eldredge's *Wild at Heart* materials became like water to a thirsty soul. His *Field Manual* guided me to deep places in my heart, to wounds that were the core roots of my struggle. Finally, I stumbled onto Jim Wilder's *Life Model* and his other writings. In them I began to learn about real maturity, what it takes to move from being a child to being a man. He also introduced me to some powerful brain science that gave credence to what we were doing in our recovery groups.

> *I still believed the lie that sex was like oxygen and that I could not survive without it.*

I even started writing my own book, *New Hope for Sexual Integrity*. Because of God's miraculous work in my life, I can humbly proclaim that I have walked in freedom (no pornography or masturbation) for almost 11 years now. I now know I don't ever have to go back. My flesh is certainly capable of returning; but God has given me a redeemed heart that is stronger than my flesh. God continues to rebuild my marriage as well. My wife and I enjoy being together, and God is showing us real intimacy and the kind of joy He intends for marriage. Thankfully, I am a living testimony to God's ability to transform, heal, and deliver.

A few of the important things my journey has taught me:

1. God does not intend us to be alone. The most important thing I did to

start walking in freedom was the very thing I was most terrified to do — tell others the truth about my struggle. Sin, especially sexual bondage, is too powerful to fight through alone. We find our way to freedom when we start being honest with others.

2. We must allow God to use our external struggles to show us the wounded places in our heart. I learned that my addiction was a symptom of deeper problems. I didn't enjoy my sexual sin; I used it as a drug to numb inner pain. When I stopped taking the pain medication, I had to face many painful things I had run from all my life. For example, I was forced to face painful memories about my father and see the ways I had allowed difficulties in that relationship to drive my addictive patterns.

I was forced to face the memories of an older boy asking me to perform oral sex on him and of being propositioned by a grown man when I was seven. These encounters had a significant impact. Remembering the events and recognizing the wounds caused intense pain; I wanted to retreat to the comfort of pornography. However, as I waited for God, as I allowed myself to weep over my pain, I experienced His healing power flowing through me. I heard Him speak His truth in place of Satan's lies. I began to discover that there was good in me, that God's Spirit was working in and through me, and this discovery gave me power and hope for each new day.

I also began renouncing vows of self-protection. I had convinced myself, you're on your own; don't let anyone see your weakness. Letting that go freed me to begin asking others for help rather than keeping them safely at a distance. I had vowed to myself, I will be seen as successful and significant. I let that go, too, which allowed me the freedom to fail and even to share my failures with others. It opened my heart to realize that even if I lost my job, even if my church imploded, I was still a beloved son of the King of kings. My worth was not connected to my performance. I discovered my identity in Christ.

3. We must be willing to see the true impact of our sin on others. Sexual bondage leaves a person emotionally numb and unavailable to those around him. Satan used my emotional disconnection to do incredible damage to my wife's heart and soul. I see this repeated over and over when I meet with new couples. The pain a husband's sin brings on his wife is profound.

One wife shared her story of growing up with an alcoholic father and of being raped when she was a teenager. When she described the day she found her husband looking at porn on the computer, she broke down in tears saying, "This hurts so much more than being raped." My heart broke for her, for my wife, and for every wife that day.

Some men struggle to understand how this pain could compare to the trauma of rape. As I understand it, God designed sexual intimacy to create a primary relational attachment. In fact, the verb Paul uses in Ephesians 5:31 for "unite" can literally be translated "glue together." Hearts glued together do not separate without great pain. Pornography detaches sex from love, and that separation causes the pain of betrayal and emotional distance.

The pain is also intense because any unhealed sexual and relational pain your wife might have prior to her finding out about your sin naturally comes flooding back in the moment of discovery. She feels the betrayal and the unprocessed pain of her past. In the moment, however, it is mingled together and all she can see is your betrayal. You have wounded her where she was already deeply wounded. Don't, however, use this as an excuse to not come clean with your wife. Disclosure will be painful; but the real source of pain is what you have done, not telling her the truth.

4. God can redeem our addiction to bring glory to Himself, blessing in our lives, and encouragement to others. I will never forget hearing my wife pray, "Lord, thank you for his addiction and for the journey of healing it has put us on." There were many broken places in both our hearts that we would not have faced if my struggle had not been so abhorrent to us. After all, in ministry, being a "workaholic" is generally rewarded. However, because I hated my particular sin and had a glimpse of how much it crushed my wife, I was willing to do whatever was necessary to find healing.

Thankfully, God also continues to use our healing journey to equip us to minister to individuals and couples on the road of recovery. We have seen lives transformed and marriages resurrected — first ours, and then many others. It puts Romans 8:28 in an   amazing new light: "And we know that God causes everything to work together for the good of those who love God and are called according to his purpose for them."

No, the path of recovery and healing will not be easy. But I can honestly tell you there is no comparison between life in bondage and life in freedom.

Pastor Darrell Brazell
*www.NewHope4si.com*
*www.NewHopeLawrence.com*

**Reflections:**

When speaking of relationships, Darrell states, "Pornography makes real connection impossible" and "Sexual bondage leaves a person emotionally numb and unavailable to those around him."

How has sexual addiction affected your relationships? _____
_____
_____
_____
_____

"The problems and neglect in my family left me hurting and looking for ways to numb my emotional pain. I learned very quickly that sex is a powerful drug."

Does this part of Darrell's story sound similar to yours? _____
_____

How? _____
_____
_____

I learned that my addiction was a symptom of deeper problems... I had to face many painful things I had run from all my life.

What are you running from or trying to cover up?_____
_____
_____
_____

Darrell prayed for God to send someone to walk the journey with him and help him be accountable.

Would you pray that same prayer right now?_____

"He (God) comforted me and showed me that what I really needed wasn't pornography, a sexual release, or even my wife's body, but Him."

This may be a new idea to you, that what you really need is God. On the following scale mark where your belief lies now:

I need porn, sex, etc.          1 – 2 – 3 – 4 – 5 -6- 7 – 8 – 9 -10

I need God.                     1 – 2 – 3 – 4 – 5 -6- 7 – 8 – 9 -10

# WHAT SECRET SINS AND ADDICTIONS DON'T TELL YOU

Your addiction wants you to believe it's your friend, your pal, your best buddy, the one you can turn to for comfort when you hurt. But that's a lie. Your addiction is your enemy, and it will always, always lie to you. That's what it does. There are several lies your addiction will constantly whisper in your ear. If you believe any of these, you will never break free from its grasp:

- *You can stop whenever you want.* If you are addicted you aren't in control. Your addictions will harm your life, family, job and friendships.

- *This will be your last time (last fling, last website, last strip club, last episode)!* That is, until the next addictive urge catches up with you – tomorrow, next week, or next month.

- *Sharing your secret sin or addiction is too costly.* You may believe that it may ruin your reputation or marriage if you're found out. You may not believe me when I tell you that keeping your addiction secret is far more painful than bringing it out in the open.

There are many people caught in secret sins and addictions (porn, prostitution, masturbation, etc.) who are truly trying to get out. They try to get free by quoting Scripture, reading the Bible, praying, and other spiritual disciplines. While all of these activities are important, the key to your freedom is this: *coming out of the closet with your secret.*

Secrets don't have to remain that way. You can be free from them. Addictions lose their power when you tell someone. Confession is bringing your deepest sins out of the darkness and into the light and sharing your need to overcome them with someone who can help.

Make a decision to live in the light, not in the darkness. In this, you will find freedom. That is what happened to a young man named Augustine born in 354 A. D.

## Augustine

Augustine, although raised as a Christian, left the church to follow the Manichaean religion, much to his mother's despair.[44] As a youth Augustine lived a lifestyle of overindulgence and sexual sin.

At about the age of 19, Augustine began an affair with a young woman. Though his mother wanted him to marry a person of his class, the woman remained his lover[45] for over 13 years and gave birth to his son Adeodatus. In 385, Augustine ended his relationship in order to prepare himself to marry an heiress at his mother's insistence.[46]

In late summer of 386, Augustine entertained a visitor who spoke about St. Anthony and others who had left all they had to devote themselves to self-denial and prayer while living in the Egyptian desert. Augustine went to his garden and wrestled with the demands of his flesh and bitterly wept over his inability to accept the challenge.

He heard a childlike voice telling him to "take up and read" which he took as a divine command to open the Bible and read the first thing he saw. He opened to Romans 13, where he read: "Not in riots and drunken parties, not in eroticism and indecencies, not in strife and rivalry, but put on the Lord Jesus Christ and make no provision for the flesh in its lusts" (verse 14).

At this moment, confidence and peace flooded into his heart and drove out the anguish that had overwhelmed him in the garden. Paul's question, "Who will free me from this body of death?" (Romans 7:24) became Augustine's question. Paul's answer, "Thanks be to God through Jesus Christ our Lord!" (Romans 7:25) became precisely the truth he had long sought. Augustine reported all this to his mother, who rejoiced in God for His answer to her lifelong prayer for her son.

> *"The confession of evil works is the first beginning of good works."*

## Saint Augustine

He later became Saint Augustine and wrote a book called *Confessions*. In this remarkably honest story of his life, he shared his past sinful lifestyle, how he slowly and painfully turned away from it and eventually became a follower of Jesus.[47] And he offers praise and thanksgiving in honor of God's glory.

He became one of Christianity's most influential thinkers, and his writings are probably more influential in the history of thought than any other Christian writer since the Apostle Paul.[48] Many readers have found inspiration, freedom and joy in reading about his life's journey from pleasure-seeking to peace.[49] I wonder if we would even have heard of Augustine if he hadn't confessed.

Healing comes through confession – first with yourself and then with another person. It means owning that "I have a problem." Believing lies will never give you the power to overcome them.[51] They only take deeper root and last longer. While facing the truth and being honest with yourself and another person may be very difficult and scary, freedom rarely occurs without it.

> ***Therefore confess your sins to each other and pray***
> ***for each other so that you may be healed.***[50]

However, please realize that not everyone is safe, and not everyone knows how to help. Be sure to share with godly people who will offer ongoing prayer, counsel, and support as you overcome. Churches often offer support groups to men overcoming similar issues as yours. Here are four reasons we should confess our sins to a *safe* person:

1. It causes us to consider the sin in our lives – hidden sin is easy to rationalize – we reduce the seriousness and ignore the consequences.

2. It causes us to seek out trustworthy people – We need to seek out and be friends with honest and loving people.

3. It encourages dependence on others – It isn't until we have seen both sides of a person and revealed both sides of ourselves that we can know and be known

4. That we may be healed – Spiritual healing comes when we confess and pray for each other.

Eventually, if you find a buddy to work with and continue to be honest with him and work through the Biblical principles listed in this book, you will find freedom through Christ. You will eventually overcome your addictions. Some day they will be a fading memory for you like they are for the men who told their stories in this book.

**Reflections:**

1. What is the most frequent lie that your addiction tells you? It may be one of the three listed above or a different one. Write it here: _____
   _____
   _____
   _____
   _____
   _____

2. How many times have you believed this lie? _____

3. List two ways that bringing your sin from the darkness to the light helps you get free. _____
   _____
   _____
   _____
   _____

4. Is there a safe and loving person of the same sex that you can confess to?
   Yes _____    No _____

   You don't need to write down the name. It's enough that you know it. Now schedule a time that you can confess to this safe person.

   Write it here: _____

# A FALL FROM GRACE

During the summer of 2012 I heard the news reports of Penn State assistant football coach Jerry Sandusky, accused of abusing many children (50 counts thus far). While I grimace with pain for Jerry Sandusky's victims, I rejoice at the courage of those who have come forward to tell difficult truths about this football coach and have made his deeds of child abuse known. These young men were the brave ones willing to give their testimony of what truly happened with this popular and well-respected coach.

The victims' testimonies remind me of a line from the movie "The Help", a movie that came out in 2011 about African-American maids working in white households in Jackson, Mississippi."[52] A mother, who remained silent about injustices going on around her, tells her daughter, "Courage often skips a generation, but I am glad you have brought it back into our family." The daughter had taken the hard, courageous step of telling difficult truths that needed to be shared.

Jerry Sandusky was sentenced to 30 to 60 years. As he was 68 years old, this sentence will put him in prison for the rest of his life.

Tim Rohan writes in the New York Times:

> Bellefonte, Pennsylvania – "Jerry Sandusky stood in court Tuesday in his current uniform, the bright red jumpsuit of the Centre County jail. No longer was he in his Penn State coaching gear, nor in the suit and tie he wore at his trial in June. He was, in a sense, as powerless before his victims as they had once been before him. So he sat, forced to listen.

> "'We both know exactly what happened,'" said one of three victims who stood and spoke. Another said: 'I am troubled with flashbacks of his naked body, something that will never be erased from my memory. Jerry has harmed children, of which I am one of them.'

"There is no punishment sufficient for you," the mother of another victim wrote in a statement read by the lead prosecutor.

"Another victim wrote: 'There is no remorse. There is no acknowledgment of regret, only evil.'

"Mr. Sandusky was convicted of sexually abusing 10 boys, all from disadvantaged homes. Mr. Sandusky used his connections to the Penn State football program, as well as his own charity for disadvantaged youths, the Second Mile, to identify potential victims, get close to them and then sexually violate them . . ."[53]

This is a picture of betrayal trauma for 10 young boys who will live with scars for the rest of their lives. My heart aches for them, and I rejoiced along with them at seeing justice served when Mr. Sandusky was finally sentenced and imprisoned.

A little over a year since Jerry Sandusky was found guilty one of Sandusky's adopted sons filed court documents to legally change his name on behalf of himself, his wife, and his four children.[54] The court documents were sealed and if granted, the motion would allow this son and his family to drop the name Sandusky and shed a public connection with the convicted pedophile.

How sad to have a father that lacks such integrity that you need to change your name to distance yourself. Here's what the Bible has to say about a good name: "A good name is to be desired above great riches..." (Proverbs 22:1, AV) and "A good name is better than fine perfume" (Ecclesiastes 7:1). Make it your goal to live in such a way that your children are proud to bear your name.

---

*The average pedophile molests 150 victims during their lifetime.*[55]
*Two thirds of all prisoners convicted of rape or sexual assault had committed their crime against a child.*[56]
*"Research shows pedophiles have a high rate of repeat offenses – with study statistics varying between 65 and 80 percent."*[57]
*"25% of all sex offenders re-offend within 15 years"*[58]

---

Jay Younts states the following, in the Shepherd Press:

> **The average pedophile molests 150 victims during their lifetime.**[59]

## Penn State and Sandusky: What about God?

"Penn State former assistant football coach Jerry Sandusky was convicted of sexually abusing 10 boys, some on campus. Sandusky was called a dangerous, sociopathic sexual predator who had previously raped, sodomized, and/or otherwise seriously harmed young boys on the Penn State campus, and who was substantially likely to continue to engage in similar conduct in the future. . . "Almost every negative term imaginable has been used to describe, first, the wanton rape of children.... And, second, the equally egregious cover-up by the PSU coaches and administration. These terms all fit the crime and greedy self-interest by those involved. But there is one word that has not been used by the media to describe these events: SIN. First and foremost, these heinous actions are wrong because they violate the law and rule of God. They are sin.

"The problem for our culture with using the word 'sin' to describe these actions is that 'sin' implies that there is a God to whom we must be accountable. Even in the face of these outrageous events, our culture, our political leaders, and our media will not call these crimes what they really are. The idea of sin means that we are accountable to God for what we do . . ."[60]

> *"The world is full of men who want to be right, when actually the secret of a man's strength and his pathway to true honor is his ability to admit fault when he has failed. God wants to fill the church with men who can say they are wrong when they are wrong. A man who is willing to humble himself before God and his family and say 'I was wrong' will find that his family has all the confidence in the world in him and will much more readily follow him. If he stubbornly refuses to repent or admit he was wrong, their confidence in him and in his leadership erodes."*

Jim Anderson, *Unmasked: Exposing the Cultural Sexual Assault*[61]

## Friday Night Football and a Culture of Rape

Internet Petition:

Here's an excerpt from a college football player's petition in 2013 that is circulating on the Internet about football and rape. All men, but especially young men, need to consider this. Research suggests that what you do in high school and college will be what you continue doing. If we start a habit of lust, porn, and using women, then we can expect that 20, 30, 40 and even 50 years later we will still have this problem.

"I'm a college football player, and my friend Carmen and I are calling on the National Federation of High School Associations to train high school coaches to prevent rape.

"On March 13, 2013 two high school football players will be put on trial in Steubenville, Ohio. They're accused of raping an unconscious girl at a party . . . And their coach has been accused of covering up the alleged crime. Some people are saying that what happened in Steubenville is part of a culture of hero worship, where star football players can get away with anything. We've seen this over and over again, from Steubenville High School up to the NFL. I'm a college football player, and I've seen it with my own eyes.

"I believe that playing sports is great for kids, and playing football helped me develop into the strong person I am today. But I cannot deny that there's a link between sports culture and rape culture, and that something must be done to fix it.

"My friend Carmen and I started a petition on Change.org asking the National Federation of High School Associations, which trains coaches in more than 18,000 high schools, to develop a training to prevent sexual assault.

"My friend Carmen has worked as a rape crisis counselor, and one thing that shocks us both is how many women blame themselves for being raped. We have got to stop blaming victims and start teaching young men that it is never okay to have sex with someone against her will. Not even if she's drunk, not even if she's your girlfriend.

> **Guys need to understand that No really means No.**

"Playing sports is a privilege, not a right — and doing so comes with responsibilities for players and for coaches. Training coaches to teach their players to prevent sexual assault is the first step to making sure that what happened in Steubenville never happens again. The National Federation of High School Associations runs trainings that reach over 11 million students, and those trainings are mandated by law in a lot of states. I know that if enough people sign Carmen's and my petition, the NFHSA will see that this is an opportunity to do tremendous good and help millions of kids. . .

"Thank you,
"Connor Clancy via *Change.org*
Waterville, Maine" [62]

You might be wondering what happened to the men who engaged in this hideous crime. Trent Mays, 17, and Ma'lik Richmond, 16, were found guilty of raping a drunken 16-year-old girl. Mays was sentenced to a minimum of two years in a juvenile correctional facility, Richmond to a minimum of one year. Both could be in detention until they are 21. Mays was also found guilty of disseminating a nude photo of a minor.

The ruling brings an end to a trial that divided Steubenville and gained media attention for its shocking text messages, cell phone pictures and videos, and social media posts surrounding the victim's sexual abuse.[63] Unfortunately, the cell phone has become a primary tool in pornography for young people.

I was deeply disturbed when I read about this woman at the party who was taken advantage of while unconscious. I then realized that our Lord saw her suffering and heard her cry of agony. Perhaps the very feelings of sorrow I was sensing were the same ones He was feeling. The Bible says "In all their distress He too was distressed" (Isaiah 63:9).

God sees the suffering of people[5] and hears their cry. He cares deeply about the woman who was mistreated by these men. He hears the cries of every woman and child who is being harmed.

I think about what happened to this woman when she woke up. What agony, pain, and long-lasting issues will she wrestle with because of this tragic incident? Chances are she will struggle with shame, guilt, and hopelessness – she might even become suicidal. Each of us needs to respond rightly when we are faced with wrong choices.

---

5    Exodus 3: 7, The Lord said, "I have indeed seen the misery of my people in Egypt. I have heard them crying out because of their slave drivers, and I am concerned about their suffering."

**Reflections:**

Has anyone ever offered you a sincere, heart-felt apology?_____

Write down what you felt. _____

_____

_____

_____

Did it make it easier for you to forgive them?_____

Why? _____

_____

_____

_____

_____

When you are wrong, can you admit it? _____ How hard is it to admit
when you have done something like this?

$$1 - 2 - 3 - 4 - 5 - 6 - 7 - 8 - 9 - 10$$

Can you call sin "sin"? _____ What other words might you use to describe it to make it sound softer and more acceptable?

_____

_____

_____

_____

_____

# DISCOVERING GRACE

by Sam

School was tough. I couldn't make friends, let alone get a girlfriend. Life at home was no better. It wasn't so much the occasional violent beatings, but more the constant anger, the continual fear, not knowing what kind of mood my dad would be in when he got home from work.

None of us really talked to each other. We were all terrified. They say family friction between siblings builds character, but there wasn't any of that in our house. We were all too afraid to speak.

As soon as I hit 16, I left home and moved to London to be an actor. I had a bit of success. Theatre. Some TV. But I couldn't hide from my emotions. I sought protection in drugs and hung out at some of Soho's sleazier night spots.

It was in these festering drug dens, visited by gangsters and low-life criminals that I was hit on by older women, mother figures. I was lonely. Wasted. Desperate to be loved and touched. Desperate for intimacy. Desperate for sex.

But the things I let these women do to me didn't have anything to do with love, or even sex. It was abuse. I see that now, but I couldn't then. And intent on punishing myself, intent on expressing my self-loathing, I kept going back for more.

I found it difficult to form relationships with girls my own age, girls I actually found attractive. If I did meet someone I liked, I messed it up. Why? Because I was a mess: I was on crack, homeless and jobless, taking whatever sex I could find. I was out-of-my-face 24/7. And when I was feeling lonely, I'd return to these women who would pay me the attention I craved. Only now, looking back, can I see the filthiness of it, the depravity.

Then I finally hit rock bottom. I fell in love with a girl, a young woman who had been raped, who was clearly working through her own issues. She broke my heart. And it was through this gaping wound that Jesus entered. I'm reminded of a few lines from Oscar Wilde's poem *The Ballad of Reading Gaol*, which he wrote while serving a two-year sentence:

> "How else may man make straight his plan
> And cleanse his soul from sin?
> How else but through *a broken heart*
> May Lord Christ enter in?"

Jesus found me while I was wandering around the streets of London, high on drugs, tripping on ecstasy and LSD. I was 27 but really, inside, I was a little boy, lost.

When I saw an older lady handing out leaflets about God, I thought it would be cool to stop and talk to her. She invited me to pray. My brother was with me and he prayed too.

A few days later it felt like I'd taken LSD, but I hadn't. All of the colors were brighter, more vivid. Birdsong became the most beautiful music ever. The moon became magical, hanging in the sky, glorious, bright. And as I sat at home on the 19th floor of my south London apartment, a Spirit filled the room: thick, tangible. I was in awe. It was stronger than being on ecstasy, more beautiful than acid. It was a hovering Spirit, gentle, comforting. I was afraid if I moved I'd frighten it away.

It was my brother who figured it out: We had been *born again*. We both felt completely new and clean. In the Bible Jesus says: "I make everything new!" (Revelation 21:5) Then Ian  realized the strange spiritual presence in my room was the Holy Spirit. I'd taken enough drugs to know it wasn't a drug high. This was much more beautiful. I suddenly knew what the phrase "the fear of God" meant. It wasn't about being afraid of God, but afraid of losing God! I wanted this Spirit to stay with me forever.

My brother had started reading the Bible, so I did too. It was one of those Bibles where the words of Jesus are in red letters. And the words became alive. They started floating off the page: "Peace I leave with you. My peace I give you. Do not let your heart be troubled, and do not be afraid." (John 14:27)

WOW!

And so I began my Christian journey. Yet even though Jesus had set me free from drugs, the sexual depravity didn't stop. I hid a secret addiction. Fifteen years later I was still secretly indulging in porn. Lonely Christmas days in London, when everyone else (at least in my imagination) was having fun celebrating with turkey and mince pies, I was holed up with a bottle of whiskey and Internet porn.

In the movie *The Perks of Being a Wallflower,* a teenage boy, recovering from childhood sexual abuse by a woman, is told by his English teacher: "We accept the love we think we deserve." Indulging in these lonely sex sessions, abusing myself the way I had been abused, was this the love I thought I deserved? Not love at all but hatred, self-hatred disguised as love. Some of us express our pain through hurting others, while some express our pain through hurting ourselves.

> ***Some of us express our pain through hurting others, while some express our pain through hurting ourselves.***

So how did I escape this black hole of despair? I knew the gospel, I believed in Jesus, but I was still locked in an addiction. Why? Why did I hate myself so much? Why was I so intent on destroying myself? Sometimes my wrists cried out to be cut. My choices were either to get my act together or to commit suicide. Sometimes I'd cry out to God: "Kill me. Take me to be with You. Anything but this. I would rather die and be with You than continue in this self-abuse, this sexual energy I can't control." And just when I thought God had already laid all His cards on the table, He played His ace.

### An Ace Called Grace

Even though I had been a Christian many years, I had never truly understood grace or how much God loved me. I mean, I'd read in the Bible that He loved me. I'd heard it preached that He loved me. But I hadn't truly believed in my heart that He loved me. Because of what Christ had done, God had forgiven me. Not only that, He had made me *holy*. To God, I was pure. I was beautiful. This was amazing!

> "By one sacrifice He has made perfect forever
> those who have been made holy." (Hebrews 10:14)

Jesus had made me *perfect forever!*

I was so excited. I started to read more about grace, and I learned that many people, all over the world, were understanding grace too. God didn't see us as sinners anymore, once we had given our lives to Him. He had forgiven us, for all our sin, on the cross, and had made us perfect in Him!

Further study taught me that, on the cross, Jesus changed places with us. He became sin, while we became holy and right with God through Him. "Christ had no sin, but God made Him become sin so that in Christ we could be right with God." (2 Corinthians 5:21, ERV). I was right with God! Paul also writes that the mystery of the gospel is "Christ *in* you, the hope of glory." (Colossians 1:27).

I learned that *glory* in the Bible means "a beauty and majesty unique to God" and *hope* means "a joyful confidence." If I were to stand on a street corner and proclaim "I have the beauty and majesty of God," I'd probably be locked up. But Paul is telling us we *can* say this with a joyful confidence. The moment we accept Christ, we are given the beauty and majesty of God! No wonder Isaiah, the Old Testament prophet, was so excited:

"I am overwhelmed with joy in the LORD my God, for He has dressed me in garments of salvation. He has draped me in a robe of *His* righteousness" (Isaiah 61:10).

And so, like Isaiah, I too was overwhelmed with joy. I wasn't dirty, depraved, and worthless – a pit of disgraceful filth fit for nothing but the eternal rubbish dump – I was draped in a robe of *His* righteousness. God had forgiven me of all my sin and given me eternal life – as a free gift.

"And this not of yourselves, it is a gift of God." (Ephesians 2:8).

Wow!

I have done so much wrong in my life. Many, many things. I've been a criminal. I've stolen. I've been arrested. I've been violent. And I can find an excuse for all of it – the pain of my childhood – but that doesn't get me off the hook. According to the law I'm still responsible for my actions. I know the difference between right and wrong. Even if our troubles are rooted in childhood trauma, that doesn't give us a get-out-of-jail-free card. We still deserve to be punished for our crimes.

Jesus, however, goes one better than giving us a get-out-of-jail-free card. He gives us a get-out-of-*Hell*-free card. Hell for me wasn't an eternal fire; it was the living moment, the return over and over again to the depth of depravity, to the abuse of my youth. One proverb in the Bible says "Like a dog that returns to its vomit, a fool does the same foolish things again and again" (Proverbs 26:11, ERV).

Yet in God's eyes, because of what Christ had done, and because I believed in Him, I was a new creation: "Therefore, if anyone is in Christ, He is a new creation. The old has gone, the new has come" (2 Corinthians 5:17). God loved me as I was. As I am. He would never stop loving me. It's so amazing I can't think about it without welling up with tears. What a God! That is how much He loves us. Not only has He forgiven all of our sin; He doesn't even remember it. "I will forget their sins and never again remember the evil they have done" (Hebrews 10:17, ERV) – if only we'll trust Him, love Him, open our hearts to Him.

God wants the best for us. He loves us as a parent loves a child. He would do anything to have us in relationship with Him – even die on a cross. It was either us or Him on that cross, and He chose Himself. Fair exchange?

You might not think you deserve saving. You might feel that you deserve to burn in Hell for the things you've done wrong. You might hate yourself. But here's the great news:  There is nothing you have done that God won't forgive, no matter how terrible, no matter how ashamed you are of it, if you are truly sorry and if you accept His forgiveness. Why does He forgive us?

Simple. He loves us. He longs for us. He would do anything to win our love in return. He's proved that He loved us by sending Jesus to die for us, in our place. Now he wants us to love Him with a free heart. If we turn to Him and accept His love, we are forgiven. Who could refuse His love, knowing what He has done for us? He stands, now, knocking at the door of your heart, waiting for you to invite Him in.

> **Not only has He forgiven all of our sin;**
> **He doesn't even remember it.**

Because I knew that nothing I could do could make God stop loving me, it seemed pointless to rebel anymore. Why keep doing wrong if God loved me regardless? I couldn't provoke His anger anymore. All His anger at sin, the sin of the whole world, was poured out on Christ on the cross. "The Lord has given full vent to His wrath. He has poured out His fierce anger." (Lamentations 4:11)

I have heard it said that all sin is rebellion towards God, and now I just didn't feel like rebelling anymore. He loved me anyway, in spite of me. His love for me didn't depend on my actions but on Christ's actions, and Christ had proved He loved me by dying in my place, taking my punishment for me. Now I was beyond words. Now I really understood that God truly loved me. He would rather die than live without me. He would rather shed His own blood on the cross than punish me! Such a loving, merciful, generous God.

So this was why grace was so "amazing"!

My addiction stopped. Occasionally the "old me" tries to pull me down again; but even if it does, God reminds me that He loves me and forgives me, that He will never let me go. I believe sin is sickness. What parent would let a sick child rot and die? A parent will do whatever it takes to nurse his or her child back to health. How much more will our loving God nurse us back into health and well-being? As Jesus says, "It is not the healthy who need a doctor, but the sick." (Matthew 9:12)

Our destiny is eternal. God will complete the work He has started in us. He is our Doctor. He is our Healer. And even if our old sinful natures do try to rear their ugly heads, His Spirit living in us is stronger. He will never let us go.

**Reflections:**

1. "We accept the love we think we deserve." The author realized that indulging in lonely sex sessions was really self-hatred disguised as love. "Some of us express our pain through hurting others, while some express our pain through hurting ourselves."

   Have you had a pattern of abusing yourself sexually? _____
   _____

   Do you recognize this as actually being self-abuse?
   _____
   _____
   _____

2. You may have read that Jesus loves you, and you may have heard it preached. In your heart do you really believe it? Why or why not? __
   _____
   _____
   _____
   _____
   _____

3. The author states: "Jesus changed places with us. He became sin, while we became holy and right with God through Him. 'Christ had no sin, but God made Him become sin so that in Christ we could be right with God.'" (2 Corinthians 5:21, ERV). Write this verse in your own words: _____
   _____
   _____
   _____
   _____
   _____
   _____
   _____
   _____
   _____

4. There is nothing you have done that God won't forgive – no matter how terrible, no matter how ashamed you are of it – if you turn from your sin and ask for His forgiveness.

   Do you believe the above statement is true? _____ If you believe it, what difference should it make in your life each day? _____

   _____

   _____

   _____

   _____

   _____

   _____

# AN ABUNDANCE OF MERCY AND GRACE

If you are reading this book, you may have been involved in sexual sin and immorality. You may have fallen into abnormal or destructive behaviors earning you the label of registered sex offender (RSO) and/or prison time.

We did not begin this way; our choices brought us here. Somewhere our decisions led us deeper into the darkness while we were grasping in vain for something to hold on to even as everything crumbled under our feet. The guilt and shame of our secret life sliced open our hearts and filled our minds with pain as we cried out, "How could I have ever done such a thing? Never, never again!" But tomorrow came, and we did it again.

When the guilt lets up, the pressure mounts, and once again we creep closer and closer to the edge of the cliff. We promise ourselves, "Just one more time, just one more look, just one more touch, and then I'll stop." But we don't stop. In fact, falling quicker, and failing and thrashing about, we fall deeper into the darkness, into the pit of despair. Guilt and shame tell us that we are all alone. We are unable to believe the truth that there is hope.

We begin climbing, once again, up and out of the pit, and by now we "know" what will help us climb. We work harder, perhaps overtime or even at a second job to help pay off the secret credit card bills, trying to treat our wife and children a bit nicer, thinking we can make up for the  mess we are secretly causing in their lives. We delete all of the pornography, even the secret files, vowing never to go back, but the images remain burned in our brains. We begin attending church (and even stay awake), or we consider joining a men's Bible study. We may pick up a Bible or a self-help book. But none of these things quenches the raging battle in our minds and hearts, calling us to return to the pit or calling us to finally confess. But confession is not an option since it would destroy our lives. So we return to the edge of the cliff "just one more time" to release the chaos raging deep in our souls.

We begin once again making excuses for our actions, "It's not that bad. I think she (he) likes it. It's only a picture. I'm teaching them about life. No one will ever know," etc. And we begin falling – again and again, into the abyss, into the ever-deepening darkness.

This is a story of a man who willingly exploited hundreds of children and young teens by seeking sexually explicit images and gratifying himself at the expense of their innocence and vulnerability and, very likely in many cases, even their lives. A man who groomed, took advantage of, and sexually harassed his own stepdaughter for nearly a decade, terrorizing her throughout her adolescence and young adulthood, preying on her while pretending to protect her. A man who stole over half a million dollars from various clients who had trusted him to manage their investments. He spent this money on his own sexual and perverse pleasures, abusing prostitutes and frequenting strip clubs and massage therapists. This man was a master liar and a manipulator. He presented himself as a godly man, a loving and faithful husband, a devoted father, and an upstanding and successful business professional, but instead he was filled with deceitfulness, corruption, and all manner of sexual depravity. A man whose sin, when finally uncovered, destroyed his life and forever damaged the lives of many others, including those who loved him. By God's mercy and grace he was sent to prison for 20 years and labeled as a sex offender for life.

However, this is also the story of an extraordinary God showing love and forgiveness in the life of this very deceitful man. It is the story of the kind of healing that is possible in the hands of an extraordinary God. This man was once a vile and despicable sex offender but now he has been forgiven of sin and given eternal life as a gift through faith in Jesus Christ. (I Corinthians 6:11)  My name is Gary. This is my story.

### The Crisis

"You're under arrest." Hardly the words I was expecting to hear at the end of a cross-country flight for a family meeting. I had expected the meeting to be difficult – an intervention perhaps – and I knew I had to change. I knew I needed help, but I wanted to remain in control and work through my addiction in my time and in my way. I was willfully blind to all of the warning signs, to the complaints I continually lied my way through. I carefully kept the cover-ups in place. It was increasingly difficult to remember my lies, however; I had finally gone too far; the dam had begun to break, and everything was about to change. I was no longer in control, and I thought I was going to drown in the flood of the truth.

When my family requested the meeting, I knew things were about to unravel, but I had no idea that everything was about to be torn apart. On the night before my arrest, I'd confessed most of my sins to my wife (which I later found out she already knew). I thought my confession would help prove my regret and allow me to remain at least somewhat in control. There were certain things – illegal things, including my collection of underage porn – which I could not and would not confess.

The family meeting began after my arrest in the conference room of the police station. I had only been charged with misdemeanor harassment, and I thought by talking things out I could remain in control. I was wrong. I profusely and tearfully apologized and promised to do everything I had to do to change, yet my wife of 15 years had heard enough of my lies and empty promises. She was filing for divorce and had requested an order of protection to keep me away from her and her adult children. I had destroyed my life and the lives of so many others with my sexual addiction.

The morning after my release from jail, I was homeless. I still had my business, so I thought I could regroup and survive, but my situation was about to get much worse. Much, much worse.

I went to my office. The investment firm had learned of my arrest and requested that I resign immediately or be fired. *I could still survive, I could find a new firm*, I thought; but once again, everything was about to get worse.

When I was arrested, my family took my laptop computer and began looking for financial records; but what they also found was my collection of underage porn and evidence that I had been stealing from a number of my clients' accounts. When I learned that they had turned the computer over to the police, I turned to my church for help.

> *I had destroyed my life and the lives of so many others with my sexual addiction.*

I met with one of the pastors, confessing *most* of my sins (except for the underage porn); but because my family attended the same church, I was asked not to return or attend any of their services or programs, including Celebrate Recovery.

In a few short days, I had lost my family (except for my parents and my brothers), my business, all of my friends, and was even banished from church. I had destroyed my life and the lives of so many others with my sexual addiction. I was 50 years old, and certain I would spend the rest of my life in prison. There was no chance to reconcile with my wife or give up my addictions – only a lifetime in a lonely prison cell. I believed I was worthless, my life was worthless, so I decided to end my own life and commit suicide. It seemed to be the only way out of the mess I had made.

But God had other plans. I will never know how God saved my life. All of the plans I made to die should have killed me. Although I had been unconscious under water for nearly six hours, somehow I had continued to breathe. When my body was discovered, I was flown to the hospital in critical condition, but alive. Three days later I woke up from my drug-and-alcohol-induced coma in the intensive care unit of a local trauma center. When I awoke and was declared "stable," I was once again arrested and taken to jail. Only this time there would be no bond, no release, and no escape. I was going to prison for a very, very long time.

## Confrontation

 My journey through the criminal justice system began in the Level 3 psych unit of the local county jail. Naked (except for a very small "modesty" towel) and alone in the suicide-watch cell, I did the only other thing I could do. I began to pray – really, really, pray–and began to listen to what God might say back to me. God had chosen to save my life, but why? I was confused, frightened, and alone. Finally, recalling some of the scriptures I had learned as a child, I began praying the 23rd Psalm, "The Lord is my shepherd...." Word for word and phrase by phrase, carefully considering and meditating on each verse.

What if the Lord, the God of all creation, was and is my personal shepherd? What if He would do all of the things He said in that psalm? I felt I was too bad. *It couldn't apply to me.* I began asking, "Why me? Look what I have done! Look who I am! Look where I am! There is no hope for me. I'm gonna die in prison. And even if I manage to get out, I'll be a registered sex offender for the rest of my life. No one will hire me. I won't be able to find a place to live. No one will even let me go to church. I will have no friends and no family." I cried until I could not cry anymore. Then I heard a still small voice in my spirit, "But you are still My child. I'm still your Father. I love you and I do have plans for you. I know *everywhere you have been and everything you have done,* and I know *everything you have yet to do."* And I began crying again, but cries of hope rather than cries of pain and fear.

Several weeks later, after I'd been moved to a regular cell, I read "The pangs of death surrounded me, and the floods of ungodliness made me afraid. The sorrows of Sheol surrounded me; the snares of death confronted me. In my distress, I called upon the Lord, and cried out to my God. He heard my voice from His temple, and my cry came before Him, even to His ears.... He sent from above, He took me; He drew me out of many waters. He delivered me from my strong enemy, from those who hated me, for they were too strong for me. They confronted me in the day of my calamity, but the Lord was my support. He also brought me out into a broad place; He delivered me because He delighted in me." (Psalm 18:4-6; 16-19, NKJV)

"He delivered me because He delighted in me." These were words I could hardly believe. Yet since my arrest in 2005 (and although I may be in prison until 2024), through the prayers of many and through the study and obedience to the Bible, I am learning each day to "Trust in the Lord and do good. Dwell in the land and feed on His faithfulness. Delight yourself in the Lord, and He will give you the desires of your heart." (Psalm 37:4-6) What would happen if I really trusted God?

I have good days and not-so-good days. My journey continues. God is doing an important work in my life as I continue learning to trust Him. I have been incarcerated since 2005, and although I once had a desire to die, now more than ever I have the desire to live. I have been given a new and abundant life. The blessings I have received are too many to list. They began flowing in and through my life when I quit striving and began thanking God. I began listening to and obeying Him and His Word, the Bible. I live each day in His grace and remember John Newton's words, "I am a great sinner, but Jesus Christ is a great Savior."

> ***Nobody can go back and start a new beginning, but anyone can start today and make a new ending.***

### Confession and Cleansing

If I can offer you any advice, it is that healing begins with an honest and complete confession of everything we have done, as difficult as it may be. If we hide certain sins and continue to cherish them in our hearts and if we don't confess everything, God will not hear our prayers. James writes, "Is any one sick [and sexual addiction is a sickness]? Let him call for the elders of the church to come and pray over him…. Confess your sins to one another and pray for each other that you may be healed. The prayers of a righteous man are powerful and effective."[63, 64] Also, "If we confess our sins, He [God] is faithful and just to forgive us our sins and to cleanse us from all unrighteousness."[65]

I quickly discovered that if I only partially confessed my sins, I was not cleansed and I remained stuck in my sin. Other Bible scriptures tell us to "get rid of moral filth".[66] The Psalmist wrote, "I will set nothing wicked before my eyes."[67] Job said, "I have made a covenant with my eyes not to look lustfully at a young girl." And there is much more that can be said. I urge you to study and examine the Bible for yourself, for it is the source of all truth.

There is hope and healing; however, it requires work, faith, and trust. I know beyond any doubt that no matter who you are, no matter what you have done, and no matter how addicted you are, there is hope and healing through Jesus Christ.

If you are in prison, contact your chaplain and begin a correspondence Bible study program though one of the ministries listed at the end of this article. I also suggest writing to Transparent Ministries[68] and asking for a free copy of "Freedom Begins Here." This is a 30-day devotional journal which I have gone through several times and which has been very helpful in my recovery and healing. It has also helped me share my faith with others.

If you are not in prison, contact a local church or find a Celebrate Recovery[69] program. You may also choose to join SAA (Sex Addicts Anonymous) or other support groups; however, I firmly believe there is no permanent healing and recovery from the sexual addiction apart from the mercy and grace of Jesus Christ. You must stay accountable to someone: a spouse, a friend, a pastor, or someone who knows all of your secrets and all of the games you play and will help hold you accountable, pray for you, and help you continue to heal. I pray for you and your recovery, but most of all that you would come to believe in Jesus Christ and trust Him as your Lord and Savior, for it is in Him that all healing begins. Sola Deo Gloria – To God alone be the glory.

> **There is hope and healing; however, it requires work, faith, and trust.**

**Reflections:**

1. Guilt and shame will whisper suggestions such as: "You are all alone, you are disgusting, and there is no hope for you." What else do guilt and shame tell you ?_____

   _____

   _____

2. Do you recognize this as a lie from the devil? Write down the truthful thoughts that you will dwell on instead. _____

   _____

   _____

   _____

   _____

3. The author said of himself that "By God's mercy and grace he was sent to prison for 20 years and  labeled a sex offender for life."  Why was going to prison God's mercy and grace for his life? _____

   _____

   _____

   _____

   _____

4. "If I can offer you any advice, it is that healing begins with an honest and complete confession of everything we have done. If we don't con-fess everything, God will not hear our prayers."  Will you do  what the author recommends?

   Yes _____   No _____

   To whom will you confess?  Write down their name _____

   _____

**Author**: Gary Hardy is a convicted thief, harasser and sex offender. For 50 years, he lived a life of duplicity and sexual immorality. Since his rescue from death in 2005 and his incarceration, he is working to rebuild what he once destroyed. He works with local churches as well as national ministries to create a safe release program for sex offenders, and help them integrate into local church fellowships. He works as a literacy and GED tutor in prison, writes a monthly devotional guide for prisoners through Exodus Prison Ministry, and has earned both a Bachelor's and Master's degrees from Louisiana Baptist University.

# FROM PAIN AND SHAME TO VICTORY

by Charles

I'm writing my journey over the past several years because I know there are other men who need to hear it. The past several years of my life have been some of the most painful, shameful, and difficult years imaginable. It's been a season I never want to pass through again, but also a season that I wouldn't want to trade because of the great benefits that I've experienced on a personal level.

I became a Christian when I was 20 years old; I also married at that age. Like most young men, I had been sexually aroused at an early age by being exposed to pornography and I masturbated to it. This continued through my high school years and even into my married life to some degree. The flame of lust having been aroused, it felt difficult to extinguish.

I became involved in Christian ministry and eventually became a co-pastor in a smaller church in the United States, then an associate pastor in a growing church. My ministry and my wife's ministry were growing, and the Lord was blessing and we were able to help others in many ways. However, our relationship with one another was not healthy. We had poor communication, argued a lot, and our sexual life suffered. I always felt I didn't measure up as a husband, father or Christian leader and in almost every other area of my life.

I knew I struggled with self-esteem issues but didn't realize to what degree or how that affected every aspect of my life. I also continued to struggle with fantasy and masturbation. I tried to overcome this problem through prayer and fasting. I read, memorized, and quoted the Bible and concentrated on the victory that Christ had purchased for me when He died on the cross. I tried everything I could think of except admitting my problem to another man. What I've just described is common among men, including Christians and even Christian leaders: secret sexual or self-esteem struggles that we try to solve on our own. We often gain a measure of victory but then fall back into them.

In 1995 my family and I moved to Phnom Penh, Cambodia, and became successful pastors and Christian leaders in the country. Nevertheless, our marriage relationship continued to suffer and I still struggled with lust and anger. In fact, before we left the U.S., I had this nagging thought in the back of my mind that if the devil were to take me out, it would probably be associated with lust and anger; eventually that's exactly what happened.

> *I tried everything I could think of except admitting my problem to another man.*

I failed morally. For a season of about a year I lived a secret life justifying sexual sins in my mind on the one hand and hating them on the other. My thought life was in turmoil as I lived the life of a hypocrite. I tried to find my way out but couldn't see any escape. I was too ashamed to confess my sins and knew I would be fired as a pastor; therefore, I just tried to solve my problem on my own.

I realize now that you can never solve these issues on your own; they always require confession to and support from others. I've also discovered that sexual sins and other habitual sins in our lives are only the surface problems. The root problems usually lie in a sense of worthlessness, rejection, and a poor self-image. A lack of communication skills is usually also a factor. Many of the problems in our marriage were a result of my personal dysfunctional way of looking at things and dealing with them.

I ended up leaving Cambodia, my family, my church, and all that I really loved in life. I hurt so many people. I was totally deceived. I believed lies and lived selfishly. I now realize I was being driven by unexpressed emotional needs that were being met in a forbidden way. I finally came to my senses and began a turnaround, slowly facing the pain, the shame and step-by-step rebuilding my relationship with my wife, children, and friends.

It wasn't easy, and truthfully I've met few men who have the courage to face what they've done. The easy way is to bail out on responsibilities and start over instead of dealing with our pain in a godly way. However, the sad thing is we take ourselves with us wherever we go. The pain, the wounds, and the unresolved issues of the soul remain with us when we start another relationship, which we hope will be better but rarely is. Not only do we bring our own baggage and our trail of wounded or destroyed relationships into the new relationship, but our new lover brings hers in as well.

As I've traveled on this journey for the past several years, there are a few key truths I've discovered I'd like to pass on to you:

> ***"We take ourselves with us wherever we go."***

1. The issues we face and struggle with are often the result of painful experiences we've had in our life. One assignment I had to do in my healing process was to evaluate whether the family where I grew up was dysfunctional (not normal). Although I had not been beaten or sexually abused, my father died when I was 10 and the atmosphere in my family was not one of openness or one that groomed me to develop relationship skills or to have a positive self-image. One counselor said that he had never counseled a man who had sexual issues who did not also have what he called "father wounds." This is huge for us men; we live with emotional wounds from our fathers, and we turn around and wound our own children.

2. Everyone has issues. Some of us deal with them better than others, some of us hide them better than others, but everyone has issues they deal with. I believe that a root issue for all of us, stemming back to the fall of Adam and Eve, is the issue of rejection. Almost every man I've spoken to deals with a sense of rejection. It drives us to work, perform, pretend, act out sexually, and live in an unhealthy way in many other areas of our lives, creating huge problems for us and our loved ones.

3. We can't solve our issues alone. God calls us to be part of a community – to relate to others in an intimate way. This starts with our life partner and flows over into relationships with others of the same sex. We are called to encourage one another, confess our sins to one another, and support one another, but we men are not good at that. No one likes to take the risk of sharing inner struggles with others for fear of exposure, shame and, for some of us, the fear of having to change. However, if we continue in the way we're going, we will, at the least, not experience the abundant life that God has for us in this life as well as eternal rewards in the future. At the worst we will self-destruct, like I did, and hurt not only ourselves but the innocent lives of our spouse, our children, and those who love us.

4. Regardless of the pain and personal identity struggles or marital issues we men may have, there is no excuse to take advantage of women, young girls or vulnerable children. There is just no excuse for this abuse.

We must be men who draw the line. Many, if not most of these women whom we take advantage of are also vulnerable and hurting. They have their own issues, and we make them worse by our sexual sins against them. If you asked them, most of them would want out of prostitution or pornography but they don't have that chance. Our bad choices and sins against them only increase that dependency.

As I said in the first paragraph, I don't share this to glory in my shame, but because I know that there are men everywhere who are crying on the inside. They struggle and want help but don't know where to go and can't overcome the shame. My desire is to use my experiences and struggles to help you overcome yours. I'm not a counselor but a friend who has walked the path and has obtained a great measure of freedom, while I myself continue to grow.

**Reflections:**

1. "Sexual sins ... are only the surface problems. The root problems usually lie in a sense of worthlessness, rejection, and a poor self-image. A lack of communication skills is usually also a factor."

   Circle your root problems in the sentence above.

2. "The pain, the wounds, and the unresolved issues of the soul remain with us when we eventually enter into another relationship, which we hope will be better but rarely is."

   How healthy have your relationships been on the scale below?

   Healthy, lasting relationships/Dysfunctional, destructive relationships

   1 – 2 – 3 – 4 – 5 – 6 – 7 – 8 – 9 - 10

3. "There is no excuse to take advantage of women, young girls, or vulnerable children. There is just no excuse for this abuse."

   Have you used any excuses in the past to justify your behavior?_____

4. Write the excuses you have used in the past to justify your behavior: _____

   _____

   _____

   _____

   _____

   _____

   _____

   _____

   _____

Do you want to be healed?"

Jesus asked this question of a sick man lying by the Pool of Bethesda. This was the place many of the sick, blind, and lame waited to be healed (John 5:6). Although healing is available, you have to want to be healed, and you have to be willing to step into a journey that leads to wholeness. Jesus is the One who gives both the healing, and the life-giving power for that journey called "recovery." You are never alone.

# SEVEN STRATEGIES FOR STRUGGLERS

In this chapter are seven strategies that will help you make that life-changing decision: Do **you** want to be free?

It can be tough starting out on a long, hard journey into unfamiliar territory. Many people wanting freedom from a sexual addiction simply don't know what to expect or what is needed to live every day in purity. This is why we have compiled "Seven Strategies for Strugglers."

Ask yourself if you really want to pursue purity with all your energy and determination. Don't make a hasty decision, because this may be one of the biggest (and toughest) decisions you'll ever make.

If you've made that decision and want to start your journey to purity we have seven helpful strategies to get you started.

### Strategy #1 – You Are Not Alone!

You are not alone... and purity IS possible!

Matthew 19:26, Jesus looked at them and said, "With man this is impossible, but with God all things are possible." (NKJV)

You may feel like you are the only person who struggles with sexually impure thoughts or actions. I assure you such a feeling is false. One thing is constant among all people: We were *all* born sexual beings. Men and women are emotional, physical, mental, and spiritual beings. Therefore, we face similar struggles when it comes to sexuality.

If you are reading this, then you probably want to know, "What is the *secret* to living every day in sexual purity?" However, I believe a more important question to ask would be "Is purity even possible?"

Most of us have struggled off and on with misusing our sexuality in some form. For some, it may be viewing pornography. For others, it may be having affairs or simply inappropriate contact with the opposite sex. Whatever the case, the reality is that we have all fallen short of the standard for purity set by God. (Romans 3:23)

In order to establish a solid foundation for living every day in purity, there must be two beliefs present:

- I am not perfect; therefore...
- I have room for improvement.

Another way to say this is "I need help being a man or woman of purity."

Purity IS possible. If you don't believe this, you will never succeed.

As you begin your journey to a lifestyle of purity, take a moment to think about these two beliefs. If they are not present in your current thinking, stop reading right now and ask God to help you understand your need for help and ask Him to give you a new hope for what may seem impossible, a lifestyle of purity.

*A strategy to consider:*

I am not the only person who struggles with living a lifestyle of purity. There is an entire community of humanity who can identify with my thoughts and behaviors.

Purity can be a reality in my daily life. I choose hope.

### Strategy #2 – Honesty and Humility

Honesty and humility are the building blocks of purity and blessing.

Proverbs 24:26 says "An honest answer is like a kiss on the lips."

Truth is the doorway to freedom. Until you are willing to be brutally honest about your struggle with acting out sexually, you will never achieve regular, daily purity. A lifestyle of purity begins with a commitment to honesty and humility.

Honesty is necessary for several reasons:

Honesty prevents damaging secrets from infecting your relationships. It keeps everything out in the open, protecting you from the anguish of a double life.

Honesty offers you a clear conscience. When you are honest, you never have to balance one lie against another, and you never need to look over your shoulder.

Honesty creates stability in your relationships. Being truthful with others creates a solid foundation for secure, lasting relationships.

Humility must also be present for purity to flourish. You must have an attitude that is willing to accept correction and admit that you need help facing your struggle with sexual temptations. In many respects, humility is the key to being honest. It takes a humble person to come clean about their addictive or damaging habits.

---

**Integrity is doing the right thing when no one is watching.**

---

James 4:6 says "But He gives us more grace. That is why Scripture says: 'God opposes the proud but gives grace to the humble.'" (NKJV)

A truly humble person becomes a strong person. The humble person knows he is weak, and he seeks the help necessary to become stronger. In humility we receive God's grace, but it is the proud who are truly weak and come to eventual ruin. (Proverbs 29:1)

A strategy to consider:

I will be honest with myself and others about the damage my sexual acting out has caused. I will not hide from my mistakes any longer.

I will be humble in recognizing my need for help. I cannot cultivate a lifestyle of purity on my own.

### Strategy #3 – Integrity

Proverbs 10:9a says, "He who walks with integrity walks securely...." (NKJV)

Proverbs 11:3a promises that "the integrity of the upright will guide them." (NKJV)

Integrity is closely tied to honesty. Honesty is the act of being truthful, and integrity is walking it out each day. Honesty occurs in a moment in time; integrity is a lifestyle of doing the right thing.

You may find it easy to be honest and upright when others are looking, but how do you act when no one is around? Are you truthful, ethical, and moral? Do you strive for excellence or do the very least that is required?

Integrity is necessary to live a lifestyle of purity. You must be willing to commit yourself to doing the right thing no matter who is watching or not watching. Integrity is a higher standard because to be a man or woman of integrity means you are living to please God, not people.

Integrity is the guide to a pure life. When you become a person of integrity, you will see purity come into your life; there is a cause-effect relationship between the two. You cannot enjoy a lifestyle of purity without integrity.

Do you truly want to live each day in purity? Then begin living each moment as if you are standing in the presence of God, because in reality... you are.

*A strategy to consider:*

I must be a man or woman of integrity if I ever want to enjoy the benefits of purity. Purity is impossible to achieve apart from integrity.

I will experience peace and joy by becoming a person of integrity. I cannot know such peace and joy apart from integrity.

## Strategy #4 – Faith

Faith means trusting in the One who has your best interest at heart.

Hebrews 11:1 asks, "What is faith? It is the confident assurance that what we hope for is going to happen. It is the evidence of things we cannot yet see." (NLT)

Without faith nothing changes. Freedoms from sexual acting out can never occur without faith. But even faith is useless if it is not faith in God, because the faith itself is not what makes the difference. What you put your faith *in* is what makes the difference. For example: Strong faith in a weak board will land you in the river. Weak faith in a strong board will get you across every time.

When you understand that Jesus can give you the spiritual freedom that He bought for you through His sacrifice on the cross, you will have to make two decisions. First, will you believe that He died for your sins to give you life? Second, will you trust Him completely with your life? The first question of faith is simple; who wouldn't want to have all their sins paid for and receive the gift of never-ending life? But the second question of faith isn't as easily answered.

Trusting God requires releasing your grip on all that you hold dear. It means believing that He has your best interests at heart and is FOR you, not against you. Faith in God is an act of your will to submit everything you have and everything you are into His care. You may hesitate to do this, but it is necessary if you want a life of purity.

---

> ### *Faith is a measure of trust, not strength.*

---

If you haven't experienced consistent freedom from your sexual acting out, chances are you have not developed an intimate faith in God. Faith is a measure of trust, not strength. God has the power to defeat any struggle, temptation, or sin we face. We, on the other hand, are weak, frail, and powerless against such difficulties. But "if you have faith as a mustard seed... nothing will be impossible for you." (Matt. 17:20) A mustard seed is very small. You don't need a lot of faith, just a little faith in the right Person – Jesus.

*A strategy to consider:*

I must have faith in God to experience ongoing, consistent purity. I must learn to release everything I have and everything I am into the hands of God, trusting that He has my best interests in mind

God is FOR me, not against me. He knows better than I do what I need. I trust Him today.

### Strategy #5 – Loving Accountability

Loving accountability: inviting blows that sharpen.

Proverbs 27:17 tell us "As iron sharpens iron, so a man sharpens the countenance of his friend." (NKJV)

Hebrews 10:24-25 says, "And let us consider one another in order to stir up love and good works, not forsaking the assembling of ourselves together, as is the manner of some, but exhorting one another, and so much the more as you see the Day approaching...." (NKJV).

You need other people. It is a fact of life. You cannot live in purity without the help of others. You can try, but you cannot live every day in sexual/ thought purity on your own. And there is no shame in this fact. One of the best gifts God has given you is the relationship you have with other Christians.

God wants you to be sharpened by the loving accountability of those closest to you. You must be willing to invite several people into your life whom you allow to offer critical evaluation of your attitudes and behaviors. You also must be free to review and challenge these people as well. This type of relationship will prove to be very helpful in living a lifestyle of purity.

Real accountability is not about gossip or shame. True brotherly love is caring enough about others to cry when they hurt, celebrate when they experience victory, and protect them when they approach danger. You are not responsible for anyone else's behavior, but you can be instrumental in helping to support and encourage a struggling brother or sister.

Are you willing to invite people into your life who will love you enough to plainly tell you when you are doing wrong? If you do not invite these people into your life, you will never experience lasting freedom from sexual sin as God desires. You must invite loving feedback that sharpens your character and strengthens your resolve against temptation.

*A strategy to consider:*

I need other people. I cannot face my struggles alone and expect to win. I need a team of people who will lovingly watch my lifestyle and correct me when I am headed for danger.

I need a handful of individuals who know everything about my specific struggle. They need to have access to my deepest secrets and my most intimate thoughts. I need people who are not afraid of making a difference in my life.

### Strategy #6 – Perspective

Perspective means keeping the long road in sight.

Matthew 6:19-21 tells us, "Don't store up treasures here on earth where they can erode away or may be stolen. Store them in heaven where they will never lose their value and are safe from thieves. If your profits are in heaven, your heart will be there too." (TLB)

It has been said that the trouble with life is that it is so daily. That is never truer than when struggling with sexual issues. Temptations are flying at you almost every moment of every day. You can hardly look out your window without being blasted with some sex-saturated message.

Pursuing a lifestyle of purity requires perspective. From time to time you must step back and look at the big picture of what you are trying to accomplish. It is important that you view your pursuit of purity in terms of a journey, not a destination.

You must also understand that a lifestyle of purity does not happen overnight. It requires practice, practice, and more practice. It is much like honing your skills as an athlete. You don't reach the Olympics after one practice session.

When you begin to view purity as a long-term journey, you will eliminate a lot of the stress surrounding your struggle with sexual acting out. You will develop a greater appreciation for your days of purity, and you will learn lessons from your mistakes along the way. Perspective creates a sort of "ease" to the process of living in purity. It doesn't make it easy, but it does help you to refocus your attention on what it takes to maintain a pure lifestyle

Live today with enthusiasm and a passion for purity, but remember you are ultimately building your treasure in heaven, not here. Today, do the right thing so that you will be rewarded in heaven.

---

**Temptation always promises but never delivers...**

---

*A strategy to consider:*

I must view my quest for purity as a journey, not as some specific destination I am to reach. By doing this, I will be continually learning and growing in my practice of daily purity.

I must keep my eyes focused on long-term outcomes so that I will earn eternal rewards in heaven.

### Strategy #7 – Persistence

Persistence means moving forward even if there are obstacles.

Philippians 3:14 says, "I press toward the goal for the prize of the upward call of God in Christ Jesus. (NKJV)

Galatians 6:9 tells us, "And let us not grow weary while doing good, for in due season we shall reap if we do not lose heart." (NKJV

If you have attempted to resist sexual temptations and walk in purity, then you know how difficult it is to maintain pure behaviors. It's hard work! You get tired, angry, stressed, and sometimes just fed up with "doing the right thing." But you also know that there is never any lasting satisfaction to acting in sexually impure ways.

Persistence is absolutely necessary in order to develop a lifestyle of purity. Perspective gives us the long-term vision, but persistence is what keeps us strong in the trenches of life. Commit to never give up, no matter how difficult the temptations become and no matter how many times you fall. Never give up!

There is one universal truth of every person living in consistent purity: They never quit. There is also another truth concerning individuals who continually fail in their sexual struggle: They eventually give up. As long as you continue to get back up and press on toward purity, you cannot be called a failure. You ARE a success if you resolve to always get up and move one step closer to God on your journey of purity.

Life is hard. Battling sexual temptations can be excruciatingly difficult. But if you decide in your heart that nothing will keep you from taking one more step forward toward purity, then you will win rewards, not only in this life but also in the life to come. You will experience peace, joy, and true satisfaction that are not possible from acting out sexually. You will finally have what temptation always promises but never delivers.

Do you want freedom? Then never, never give up!

*A strategy to consider:*

I must never give up on my goal of purity, no matter how many obstacles and setbacks I might face. I will develop a mindset of persistence and continue moving forward to purity.

I will acknowledge that life is hard and temptations are difficult, but that won't keep me from the true satisfaction that can be mine through a lifestyle of purity.

Jonathon Daugherty[6]
Be Broken Ministries, Inc.
*www.Bebroken.com*
*www.puresexradio.com*

---

**If porn is a gateway drug, let's close the gate.**

---

6   This article is adapted from Jonathon Daugherty's article titled: First 7 Days for Strugglers http://2.bebroken.com/first-7-days-for-strugglers.html

**Reflections:**

1. Do you believe that purity can be a reality in your daily life? _____

_____

_____

_____

2. What does it mean that your pursuit of integrity is a journey, not a destination? _____

_____

_____

_____

3. What can you do to be better at humility? _____

_____

_____

_____

_____

4. What can you do to be better at honesty? _____

_____

_____

_____

5. "As long as you continue to get back up and press on towards purity, you cannot be called a _____. You ARE a _____ if you promise to always get up and move one step closer to God on your journey of purity."

Will you make this commitment now and ask God to help you?_____

_____

_____

_____

# A BOY WHO BECAME A MAN

by Glen

When I was around 13 years old, I went to a Christian conference with my mother. It started out as a lot of fun. We sang songs, learned about God, and went on walks through the countryside. At night we stayed in dorms, mostly of 6 to 8 people, but there was one room with only a bunk bed in it so I decided to take that one. After the meeting that evening I returned to the room and was surprised to find a guy about 30 years old. I was a little embarrassed, but he seemed friendly enough. As we changed clothes, he didn't cover his private areas. As a young man just entering puberty, whose father had never spoken to him about sex, I was curious.

He started talking about his girlfriends, and before long he was talking about sex. I was fascinated. No man had ever talked to me about such things. One thing led to another, and before I fully realized what was happening he had sexually abused me. It was exciting, terrifying, and confusing. He reassured me that it was not a "homosexual thing," but just normal man-to-man stuff. The next night the same thing happened.

That experience really screwed me up. I couldn't tell my mother or anyone at the conference because I felt guilty and I felt terrible. Since I had gotten aroused by what happened, I assumed it was my fault and that I was a bad person. I was confused about my sexuality. Was I gay or straight? Had he made me gay? I tried not to think about it, but then it made me anxious about any relationships with men. Would they try the same thing?

I felt more comfortable around women than men, and I had many girlfriends but I got confused about whether I wanted them to be my lovers or my friends.

As a young man I felt I needed to be strong and not show any weakness, so it took a long time before I realized that good counseling could help, especially group work. It took me 20 years before I felt comfortable talking to my pastor about what had happened. He was understanding, but not very sympathetic. Since then I've done several years of counseling and prayer, and I'm still recovering at age 52.

I am married, but sometimes I feel like this man who abused me is in bed with us trying to destroy our marriage. Even while married, I have sometimes felt it easier to seek comfort in porn or to withdraw into myself than to seek help.

However, lately I believe more strongly than ever that healing of victims and victimizers is really possible. For men it is possible through fellowship with other men who are struggling and through believing in the grace that only God can provide.

I am not alone. I have met many men who have been abused by people who should have been protecting them – pastors, priests and Christian men, some of them married. The effects of this are often that they lose their faith and turn against those of faith. I understand why this happens, but it makes me sad that the blame is put on God and that the victim turns away from the one Person who can bring healing and restoration.

I genuinely hope that if you are reading this, you also experience this healing and restoration in your life. No one is too far gone to receive the love of God. It is possible to be in a successful non-abusive relationship. I am now involved in ministry to those who have been abused and to some who have been abusers. Both of them are longing for intimacy.

Not many are brave enough to take the steps that could lead to their healing. We try to convince ourselves that we are a "special case," but we all have choices to make and we can choose the path that leads to restoration, which is surely the more difficult path but at the end of which we will find real healing and restoration.

> **God says that YOU are precious and He loves you
> no matter what you have done.**

I believe that God's grace is so big that there is no place so deep that He cannot reach. You may feel that your life is out of control, but it can come under control again with faith and with help. The world says to some of us that we are worthless, un-healable and hopeless. God says that YOU are precious and He loves you no matter what you have done. The more we realize that, the more we can turn away from the things that bind us. But we can't do it alone. I encourage you to find an organization or church that can help you to make good choices that will help you (and those you love).

**Reflections:**

1. "I have sometimes felt it easier to seek comfort in porn or to withdraw into myself than to seek help. Is this true or false in your own life? Circle your answer: True or False

2. I have met many men who have been abused by people who should have been protecting them. Has someone betrayed you whom you should have been able to trust?_____

3. Write out a prayer, from your heart, of forgiveness towards those you should have been able to trust: (We don't forgive those who sin against us because they *deserve* it, but for the freedom it brings.) _____

   _____
   _____
   _____
   _____
   _____

4. "No one is too far gone to receive the love of God."

   Agree or disagree? _____

   Why? _____
   _____
   _____
   _____
   _____
   _____

5. "I believe that God's grace is so big that there is no place so deep that He cannot reach." Does this include you?_____

   _____

# A MESSAGE OF HOPE FOR JOHNS

Statistics tell us that you have come from all walks of life: some of you may be professional men, police officers, pastors, Boy Scout leaders, stock brokers, military men, retirees, and even sport coaches. Many of you are married or have a partner. Some are lonely; others are thrill seekers.

Some who pay for sex do so because they dislike women and see them as an object to be abused. A number of you dislike feminists and empowered women altogether. You often see buying sex as an acceptable outlet for men's urges, buying sex as an exploit, thrill, or hobby. You often start with porn, then drink to get up the nerve. Some of you take Viagra.

And you consider yourself a good person.

Yet there is another side to sex-for-sale – a side often not seen or explored by the men who buy sex for adventure or hobby. Here's some info you might find interesting:

In the United States the average age to enter prostitution is 13 to 14 years old. Each of these children is someone's precious daughter, or even son.

Many times the men and women who sell their bodies were physically or sexually abused as children. Some who stay in prostitution do so to avoid poverty and to help their families financially. Some are homeless. They often do not choose prostitution and would not wish this job on their worst enemies; they wish only that they themselves could break free.

Many of the women experience post-traumatic stress disorder. PTSD is a mental health condition that's triggered by a terrifying event. Symptoms may include flashbacks, nightmares, and severe anxiety, as well as uncontrollable thoughts about the event. Because they live in almost constant terror, prostitutes are shaking and fearful. "Few activities are as brutal or as damaging to people as prostitution. 60-75% of the women in prostitution were raped, 70-95% physically assaulted, and 68% met the criteria for PTSD in the same range as combat veterans and victims of state-organized torture."[71]

Women in the trade are well advised to have a planned escape route for any and every client they serve. They are told to check for knives, hand-cuffs, or ropes and not to wear necklaces, because they may get stran-gled. This is willful violence, as men's sexual addiction grows, sex becomes darker, perverted and violent. Prostitutes must endure this as part of their job and no one would choose this, no one.  And they live under a constant threat of contracting AIDS or an STD. STD is defined as "any of various diseases or infections (as syphilis,[72] gonorrhea, chlamydia, and genital herpes) that are usually transmitted by direct sexual contact.  These are the side effects of the sex trade. No wonder sex workers often either feel dead inside or live in a constant state of debilitating fear.

If you are a john, you are contributing to the debilitating side-effects associated with sex work for women in the sex industry.

### Looking Deeper

Johns never *really* look into the eyes of the women they "date," or pur-chase. What they don't see is their clients' never-ending need to *scrub away* the effects of this dark lifestyle on their body or soul, shower after shower, without any lasting effect. Often they are forced into doing acts they are ashamed of —- many times a day.

---

*Women and children should never be bought or sold for any reason.*

---

Pedophiles are those who enjoy having sex with children. Yet, pedo-philia is a dark, dark, driven perversion.  Children as young as five are forced to have sex many times a day. These same children are rotated around to different cities every three to four weeks to keep them hidden.

Norma Holding, the Executive Director of SAGE,[73] tells this story:

"Many of the women and girls we work with have been gang-raped. They've experienced gang rape at thirteen and fourteen years of age. They've been arrested over and over again for prostitution... They've been recruited by pimps and traffickers all over the United States and sometimes outside the U.S. And... these are children!"

"The situation of being in prostitution is the same as being a bat-tered woman. The violence that she experiences is normalized."[74]

Yet violence should never seem normal. It is far better to work on a good and lasting relationship where you will not be adding to someone's suffering.

## An Eye-Opening Experience at School

John Schools started in 1995 in San Francisco, California, with the goal of bringing education and intervention to the johns. More than 5,000 men have gone through the school, now found in 12 states with 48 locations.

The focus is often on the experiences and harms of prostitution, such as the violence associated with soliciting, the risk of sexually transmitted disease, and the effects of prostitution on families and communities.

"Residential . . .areas are also subject to problems associated with prostitution. Community groups argue that prostitution creates traffic congestion, noise, litter, harassment of residents and declining property values . . ." "Family members of individuals who visit prostitutes may also be adversely affected. An individual who frequents prostitutes will deplete money that would otherwise be circulated within the family. Moreover, infidelity may lead to contracting communicable diseases, to the break-up of the family and, at the very least, distrust and emotional suffering."[75]

If you're thinking about visiting a prostitute, think again, as police take prostitution seriously. If a john gets caught with a minor, the charge is statutory rape – a 12-month minimum stay in a state prison.

Teachers also share the photos of diseases involved in prostitution: diseased, infected penises and vaginas filled with infections caused by STD and HIV (Human Immunodeficiency Virus that causes AIDS).[76]

The schools discuss the heart-wrenching stories of having to tell wives and partners once they have passed on their sex-related diseases which can also destroy homes and families, the lives of people who are very dear to them.

The program is not designed to blame or shame the men. It is meant to give eye-opening information that most likely was not considered before the men stepped out on a "date" for what they thought would be a thrilling adventure with a lady of the night.

If you're thinking about visiting a prostitute, think again. If a john gets caught with a minor, the charge is statutory rape -- a 12-month minimum stay in a state prison.

### Potential!

No one is born good. We *all* are born with a fallen nature –- going way back to our original ancestors, Adam and Eve.[79] The Bible says that all of us have sinned or "missed the mark" of living a perfect life.[80] But how does someone overcome seemingly irresistible urges and addictions to become the people they want to be? We all have to start somewhere.[81]

Compare this with the ineffective, often-repeated promises that we make over and over to ourselves (or others) to change by our own will power, gritting our teeth and trying harder – again. Much like a New Year's Eve resolution that is often repeated yet rarely accomplished.

> *Sin ties us up with chains,  and Jesus gives us*
> *the power to break free.*

Your desire (a personal willingness) and God's power are the keys to change. You must desire change and go through the steps needed to become a changed man or woman. Then when that desire is combined with God's power, through Jesus Christ,[82] change happens.

Here are also some practical steps to changing and becoming what can be called "a godly man". Remember, a man of good character is not made overnight.

The first step to permanent change is to become a son of God through Jesus Christ as Savior and Lord. It is then you become His child and can freely receive all He has for you (including His daily power and strength). There are prayers,[7] to help you in this beginning step, if you have not yet made this life-changing decision.

> *Your desire and God's power are the keys to change.*

Next, *dream again* – what was it that made you dream when you were growing up? What did God create you for? Thinking about these questions and asking God to give you answers can be a key to a new outlook of hope. He has good plans for you. Set your goals for a good and prosperous future.

*"For I know the plans I have for you," declares the Lord, "plans to prosper you and not to harm you, plans to give you hope and a future"* (Jeremiah

---

7    Prayers are found in: *A Man's Ultimate Destiny: A View from Heaven.*

29:11) Godly character, honesty, and integrity are built with time. You will become a godly man when your desires change within you. Our actions eventually follow our thoughts, whether good or bad.

"Sow a thought, reap an action. Sow an action, reap a habit. Sow a habit, reap a character. Sow a character, reap a destiny."[83]

These words might be modified to say:

"Sow a habit, reap an addiction. Sow an addiction, reap a character. Sow a character, reap a destiny."

We are defined by our character.

Ask God to help you despise a life of sin and instead hunger for God's Word and His ways. This can happen! Men who have been on the journey longer can tell you that those hounding, tormenting thoughts and impulses will eventually leave and not be part of your thought patterns anymore. Some will say that they are rarely tempted by those desires like they used to be. God has replaced them with healthy goals and desires.

The Bible tells us to "flee from youthful lusts," but it also tells us to pursue righteousness, faith, love, peace....[84]

You are now on a different path, searching for God and a godly lifestyle. Every man of God needs to develop a close relationship with the Lord and other Christians. The Bible gives the example of God being a large Vine and we are the branches joined to the Vine.

We need to stay "attached" or connected to Him. If the branch becomes disconnected from its life source, it will wither and die.

It is here in this connection with the Lord that we are made strong and have our thoughts and desires changed. Having a regular prayer time, worship, and Bible study helps us stay connected to the Vine. Joining a men's fellowship will help you stay connected and growing with other men.

> **"I am the Vine; you are the branches. If you remain in Me and I in you, you will bear much fruit; apart from Me you can do nothing."[85]**

Live a life of integrity – run (run!) away from deceit. Lay aside every sin that would pull you away from your Christian life – drugs, strong drink, immorality – and avoid ungodly people as friends. Run from violence. Run away from pornography.

Pat Robertson, Chancellor of Regent University,[86] tells us how he quit drinking. He poured his expensive alcohol down the drain.[87] "That was a definite break for me. From that moment on, I was not going to drink anymore. You need to make a total break. That means you should get rid of anything you have that might tempt you.

> ***Real freedom is the power to do what you should do,
> not what you want to do.***

"You must confess that you have been doing something you consider wrong, and that you have been defiling the temple of God[8]" (In the Bible, our spirit is considered the temple of God. 1 Cor. 6:19, 20). Tell God that you want and need His forgiveness and help. Command the spirit of alcoholism (or even a spirit of pornography) to leave your body in Jesus' name and "resolve that, with God's help, you will never again smoke another cigarette, another joint, of marijuana, or whatever it may be that you are giving up." "I do not believe in gradually tapering off of cigarettes, narcotics, or alcohol."[88] See the prayers at the end of this book to further assist with this cleansing process.[9]

Next, get new friends. Find Christians who have given up the same habit, to help you during the first days of quitting. Don't go back to places that would tempt you. Stay in God's presence. Replace what has controlled you with more of God.

> ***By being the master of yourself, you are the master of your fate.***

### Further Goals

If you are single, ask God if you should find a godly partner. Ask about the timing. If you are married, make it your heart's desire to become a godly husband. A man of God keeps his marriage vows and loves and respects his wife. He leads his wife and family in devotional times, prayer, and other spiritual activities. Lead by example to show your spouse how to submit to each other. Put your spouse's needs above yours. For a marriage to work,[89] both people must submit to or prefer the other, in love.[90] Lastly, forgive

---

8   If you have invited the Lord Jesus to be your Lord and Savior, repenting of your sins, He comes to live within you as Immanuel or "God with us." You become a temple of the living God and God lives within you now!

9   Prayers are found on page 239.

when necessary. Let go of small issues in order to make the marriage work. These are necessary steps toward growth and maturity. Keep Jesus Christ in the center of your marriage or single life.

Eventually, you will be able to guide and teach younger men in the Lord's ways, passing on what you have learned. For instance, the Apostle Paul, a New Testament writer, was an ungodly and angry man, throwing Christians in jail and even having them killed.[91]

Be a mentor, especially in the very things you have overcome. It's been said that "Your mess is your message," and that's true. You can effectively help others in whatever you have overcome.

**Reflections:**

1. Reread the first three paragraphs of this chapter and circle anything that describes you or your actions.

> "Sow a thought, reap an action.
> Sow an action, reap a habit
> Sow a habit and reap an addiction.
> Sow an addiction, reap a character.
> Sow a character, reap a destiny."

2. I'm sure you can think of negative examples in your life where this has been true. It takes at least 30 days to form a new habit. What old habit are you going to give up? _____
   _____
   _____
   _____
   _____

3. You defeat this habit by refusing to think about it, and you prepare to do that in advance. Write down several tempting thoughts that you will immediately replace with non-tempting thoughts when they pop back in your head (and they will).

   a. _____
   _____

   b. _____
   _____

c. _____

_____

Another way to say this is: "You can't keep a bird from landing on your head, but you can keep it from building a nest in your hair."

4. "Your desire and God's power are the keys to change." You can't do God's part, and God won't do your part.

What is God's part?_____

_____

_____

_____

What is your part?_____

_____

_____

_____

# PORNSCAR

by Richie Cruz

My first exposure to pornography happened when I was six years old on the playground. I can still remember the image to this day. That image hijacked my naïve six-year-old mind and was the impetus that gradually shaped a life of addiction, isolation, and duplicity.

Seasons of resisting porn were outweighed by seasons of a more progressive form of porn addiction, and with it increased isolation and duplicity. Being a pastor's kid didn't help my situation either. Too ashamed to talk about my struggles with anyone, especially my dad, I was left alone to fight my battles.

### The Downward Spiral of Porn

This struggle continued all through my childhood and into adulthood. In fact, this secret addiction eventually spilled over into my marriage. My wife had caught me looking at porn on several occasions. Fearful of what she would do, I promised that I would never look at it again, only to be overcome with my craving for harder and grosser forms of pornography.

Five years into our marriage, images on a screen no longer satisfied me. Succumbing to my lust, I eventually contacted a lady selling her "services" on Craigslist and with $100 fulfilled the porn fantasies that had brewed in my mind for decades.

Years of shame and years of struggling alone, with no one to talk to, finally became too overwhelming. I was at the lowest point I had ever been in my life and had, at last, recognized my depravity. I needed help.

It was in this very pain and spiritual decadence that God met me. His truth, mercy and grace, along with the love of my family (especially from my wife) became the very thing God used to restore my marriage and purity, ultimately setting me and my family on a path to see others set free from porn and its devastating effects.

Part of what that looks like is having started an organization called Porn Scar. We host yearly gatherings where we equip and educate the church and general public about the effects of pornography including its link to sex trafficking. We also have a social media campaign that does the same.

We're called Porn Scar because we believe that "every scar has a story," and that sharing *your* story has the potential to bring healing and hope to someone who hears it.

> ***Every scar can have a redemptive story.***

I also regularly mentor other men who are recovering from pornography addiction. My hope is to help them find the tools that will bring them through their unique journey to wholeness. One of the first pieces of wisdom that I regularly share with them is, "Find out *'the why'* for *'the what.'*" Once men realize that pornography addiction is a symptom of a deeper issue they find hope and freedom. I also remind them that porn addiction is "an activity of the lonely." In other words, "Do the opposite of what you've been doing (isolation) and Get into Community. Get vulnerable. Get transparent. Get raw and real. Get whole."

> ***Find out the Why for What you were involved in.***

by Heather Cruz

My name is Heather Cruz. I've been married to my husband, Richie, for 10 years. We have had a wonderful marriage and have five children, but before we were married my husband got addicted to pornography. He got into this habit in his later elementary school years. He hid it from his family and told no one. As he got older his addiction to viewing pornography worsened.

He became extremely ill during his freshman year in college, began pursuing God more, and quit looking at porn for a few years. When he turned 23 we were married. His old addiction started to tempt him, and he gave in to viewing porn and calling the phone sex lines once every few months.

### The Confession

The only way I knew he was looking at pornography was because every time he'd fall, he'd confess it to me. I'd feel hurt, cry, call my mentor and ask for prayer, then forgive him (because it was every man's battle, right?).

After we had been married about five years, I thought my life was perfect with my husband—my best friend. But lying in bed one night he said he needed to tell me something: he told me he had been with a prostituted woman who offered sensual massage.

My heart sank. He cried. I hugged him. Then I got extremely angry and called the police. He could've given me a disease; he could've given me a deadly disease! I called a mentor the next day, and she said her husband had battled with sex addiction and that my husband needed help.

## The Change

I was aghast, disgusted, and questioned if I needed to leave my husband for my health's sake. I decided to call a couple more mentors and ask what I should do. They both told me to pray. So, pray I did. I joined a house of prayer and prayed every Monday night for the next six months.

During this time my husband began to listen to all of the Covenant Eyes podcasts. Soon after he started a men's accountability group and also a ministry called Porn Scar.[92]

I believe the greatest thing that helped bring healing to me and to our marriage was and is prayer.

I also believe if it wasn't for my husband's genuine repentance we wouldn't be together today. Richie and I have always been real close and able to talk to each other about our true feelings. I would open up to him often if I felt afraid that he was going to look at porn again. I would share with him if I felt angry or sad.

I held onto promises from God's Word.

## The Compassion

Two things brought understanding for what my husband was going through. First was knowing how the male brain is wired. Viewing pornography actually changes how men's brains work. Pornography hijacks the proper functioning of a man's brain and the effect on his thoughts and life is long-lasting. Pleasure hormones are released creating new patterns in the brain's wiring. Viewing porn creates a demand in the brain for more porn in order to achieve the same level of pleasure in the brain. As William

M. Struthers of Wheaton College explains, "Porn is a whispered promise. It promises more sex, better sex, endless sex, sex on demand, more intense orgasms, experiences of transcendence."[93]

The second reason I was able to find compassion was that I remembered that I had been set free from addictions before we were married, and Richie wasn't able to be set free from his addiction until after we were married. This helped me to show mercy to him.

I had known the shame of addiction — not addicted to viewing pornography myself but addicted to being pornography with skin on in High School. I was extremely hurt by teenage boys and young adults who had an addiction to pornography. This hurt had led me to have an alcohol and drug addiction, eating disorders, two abortions, and post-traumatic stress syndrome. Christ healed me from this at the age of 18 when I began to believe He was real, received prayer, and went through a Post-Abortion Healing Course.

When Richie had fallen I had become down but not as depressed as I was before I had met Christ. I had walked through much inner healing a few years before we married, so I had many tools to help me self-talk and figure out what was going on with me and what I needed to do to get help.

One of the greatest tools I have learned and practice is to bring everything into the light. I deeply believe that if we confess our sins to one another we will be healed.

"Therefore confess your sins to each other and pray for each other so that you may be healed. The prayer of a righteous person is powerful and effective" (James 5:16).

I am thankful for everyone who spoke into our lives, our marriage and for those who believed in us. I am thankful that we didn't go through the healing process alone and am glad that addiction to pornography is something that every man doesn't need to battle for the rest of his life. On this journey I have also learned that many women also battle with viewing pornography. There is hope and healing in Christ and community.

I encourage anyone who has any kind of addiction, or has been abused by pornographic acts in any way to reach out to someone who loves you and whom you know you can trust. Know that no matter what you have looked at or done, or what has been done to you, you are lovable.

Richie and Heather Cruz
*http://pornscar.com*

> **I am thankful for everyone who spoke into our lives,
> our marriage and for those who believed in us.**

## Reflections

1. Richie was exposed to porn at a very young age. He said the "image hijacked my naïve six-year-old mind." It led to a life of addiction, isolation, and duplicity.

   At what age were you exposed to porn? _____ What have been the results in your life? _____

   _____

   _____

   _____

2. Richie states that "images on a screen no longer satisfied me." Porn users need more porn and more stimulation to feel the same level of excitement. On a scale of 1 - 10 how close are you to acting out your fantasies in real life?

$$1 - 2 - 3 - 4 - 5 - 6 - 7 - 8 - 9 - 10$$

3. Richie recognized both his brokenness and his need for help. He says at this low point, God met him. Some people believe they have to have their act together for God to pay them any attention. What do you believe and why?_____

   _____

   _____

   _____

4. Richie's wife says, if not for her husband's genuine repentance, they wouldn't be together today. Is this true for you as well? Write what your steps will be _____

   _____

   _____

   _____

   _____

# SECTION II

## From the Hearts of Women

For someone to make a purchase there must be a product.

Perhaps you never stopped to think what it feels like from a woman's perspective to be purchased for sexual pleasure – a product to be consumed and then discarded.

The stories in this section show what it's like from the viewpoint of a prostitute, a trafficked victim, a porn star, an abuse victim and women whose partners are caught in the web of porn. This is the other side of the story. . .

# TIME TO DANCE

I had a dream. The Lord came to me and said, "I want you to meet My friends."[94] I was excited because I thought I was going to meet Isaiah, Peter or Moses. He took me by the hand and we flew loop-de-loops through the sky like we were in a cartoon. Even though we were extremely high above the ground, I was so aware of not being afraid; I loved just holding His hand and feeling the wind on my face.

Suddenly His countenance changed. He set His face intently toward Earth and we started heading directly toward the ground in a head-first dive. I thought, *Surely we aren't going to hit the ground.* But when I looked at His face, I could see fierce determination in His eyes.

> Therefore I have set My face like a flint;
> And I know that I will not be ashamed.
> Isaiah 50:7

I knew He had already decided what He was going to do. He was not going to turn around. I felt horrible dread come over me as we kept descending, even though I was holding His hand.

We didn't crash. We exploded right through the ground like a scene from an action movie. I could see the impact as we blasted through the ground. I could hear the earth exploding around us as we traveled through rock, water, and burning fire. The sound was deafening, like the sound of a rocket being launched.

I felt the earth pounding my head and rattling my body, and I could feel my skin burning and tearing. I was in immense pain in my dream, yet the Lord's face never turned to the left or right; His eyes were fixed straight ahead.

Suddenly we burst through the other side of the Earth.

I stood there looking at my body for a moment, in shock at what had just happened. My skin was lacerated. My body was weak and aching. I was crying because I was in so much pain. I thought, Surely He sees how badly I am hurt and how badly my skin is wounded and torn…Jesus was aware of my pain, but He made it known that it was not about me. He said to me, "I want you to meet My friends."

He began walking. As I followed Him, I noticed that we were in a very crowded place. I knew it was India. There were little children everywhere who were suffering. I saw some lying on the ground with flies crawling on their skin. As they passed from their horrible circumstances into the next life, He was there for each one the moment they awakened in eternity.

I saw beautiful young girls in cages; He continually stood with them. The Lord calls these seemingly forgotten ones His friends. Not one of them is forgotten in His eyes. The sadness of what I was seeing, along with the agonizing pain my body felt, left me in tears.

The Lord came over to look me in the eye. I thought He had finally noticed my pain and was coming to comfort me. Instead, He revealed my self-centered response and invited me to feel His heart: "Until your heart is torn like your flesh is now, you do not know how I feel about My friends."

He wanted me to feel the pain of the cuts in my skin so I could understand how His heart is torn. I saw children dying, mothers taking their last breath, young girls being sold, and disease spreading. It was more than I could handle. He said again, "Until your heart is torn like your flesh is now, you do not know how I feel about My friends. You do not know Me."

As I looked at the staggering injustice all around, to my surprise, He came near me to reveal His secret weapon against it. He whispered, "It is time to dance."

He began a rhythmic, tribal stomp. His perfect feet with their scars of passion were bringing justice by stomping out the injustice done to His friends. He said again, "Until your heart is torn in two, you do not know how I feel about My friends. You do not know Me."

**Reflections:**

1. Give the first word that comes to your mind when you think about these children in India. _____

   _____

   _____

   _____

2. In this dream the Lord wanted to show Julie her lack of compassion for those who are suffering. Could you too, lack compassion? _____

   _____

   _____

   _____

   _____

   _____

   _____

If you're a john , or thinking about purchasing sex, here's a snap shot of what's really going on with that woman who seems to be "enjoying it" so much . . .

## SEX TRAFFICKING IN AMERICA: ONE WOMAN'S STORY

by Mark Ellis

She grew up poor, in one of the decaying mill towns of Massachusetts. After she ran away from home, she was groomed and finally drawn into the dark world of sex trafficking, a virtual prisoner in one of the most free and prosperous countries in the world.

"I was conceived in a violent rape, so I always felt like I was worth less than other people," says Darlene Pawlik, author of "Testimony: the Dark Side of Christianity." The rape was so brutal her mother didn't talk about it for two years. She actually married the perpetrator, who continued to brutalize her.

Sexual violence seemed to follow Darlene. "From toddlerhood I was physically and sexually abused by my biological father. He used drugs and he used repressive techniques, teaching us to lie about what was going on."

Her mother's second husband took them to church occasionally, but it was more for a social connection. "At six or seven I accepted the Lord, but there was no discipleship going on. I didn't know how to follow Him."

Darlene ran away from home after her mother's second divorce. "I quit school at the end of the sixth grade," she says. "I lived as a transient in the streets, stayed in basements, or slept in cars. I slept in the store '24' for a number of months." At times a world almanac was her only pillow.

She says her mother looked for her, but didn't get much help from the local police in Haverhill, Massachusetts. "Some of the police were using my runaway friends," she alleges.

When Darlene was 13, a "handsome" man calling himself 'Ace' showed up in town, driving a black Cadillac with a crimson interior. He struck up conversations with Darlene and her runaway friends, slowly building their trust. "When the weather got cold we would get in his car and we would talk and joke around," she recalls.

Ace was patient, slowly grooming the girls for his vile purposes. "He made very few references to sexuality at first, but then he started getting into it more and more."

Darlene began using drugs such as Valium, marijuana, and alcohol – anything she could get her hands on. "I viewed (Ace) as a way I could get what I wanted and I didn't think I was worth anything anyway," she says. Her relationship with Ace turned sexual, which led to the next step in his sordid plan.

On Darlene's fourteenth birthday she was peddled into the world of sex trafficking. "That's the first time I was sold to a businessman from a neighboring town. He was absolutely thrilled I was so young."

Some of her clients included professionals, politicians, and everyday joes. "Often it was a routine thing that happened," she says, referring to the sexual encounters. "But just as much it was violent. I was gang-raped, kidnapped, beaten and brutalized. I attempted suicide many times, overdosing on pills; I tried to throw myself off a building; I tried to hang myself in a cell. I must have had angelic or Holy Spirit intervention, because I should not be alive."

Ace sold her to a man named Rac, for his exclusive use. Then Rac sold her to a small-time organized crime figure, involved with loan-sharking and gambling. The man found her an apartment in the city, while he lived with his wife and children in the suburbs.

"I was held as a house pet for a 'sugar daddy,' but there was nothing sweet about it," she notes.

When Darlene unexpectedly became pregnant, the mobster was enraged. "He told me if I didn't have an abortion he would kill me. One of his flunkies was my former pimp who had beaten me up and raped me so I didn't doubt it." He forced Darlene to make the appointment for an abortion in his presence.

As the pressure mounted, Darlene remembered the faith of her childhood, which had been dormant for so many years. "God, if you're real, I need you to help me!" she cried out when she was alone. "I don't know what to do."

That night something unusual happened. She had a vivid, Technicolor dream about the abortion process from the vantage point of the womb.

Jolted by her God-inspired dream, Darlene called a social worker she met when she first lived on the streets. She reached Marilyn Birnie, founder of Friends of the Unborn, who told her she would provide a place of refuge for Darlene – a home for unwed mothers.

Darlene spontaneously devised a plan to flee – using the pretext of a faked abortion. "I pretended to go and have an abortion and after the procedure I pretended to be in pain. I went to the bathroom a lot and cried a lot. I was terrified he would find out so I was shaking. He believed me and let me go."

She credits Marilyn Birnie with saving her life. "She didn't just save my life, she saved my children's lives and who knows how many generations."

At the home for unwed mothers, she finally found the missing piece to her Christianity. "Marilyn taught me how to be a Christian, to read the Bible every day, to talk to God every day. If there was an actual conversion experience, it was at her home. She saved my life and my destiny."

In 1990 Darlene married Mark Pawlik, sales manager for an industrial equipment company. The relationship was slow to develop and rocky at first, due to the trauma she survived and her lack of self-worth. "I felt like I wasn't good enough so I pushed him away."

In the last few years, Darlene has been very active in pro-life causes in New Hampshire. She has five children and two grandchildren.

"I want to give back to the pro-lifers who saved me," she says.

Mark Ellis
God Reports, Founder
*www.Godreports.com*

**Reflections:**

1. If you have a daughter, picture her at age 11 trying to survive on the streets. Write down what you think a typical day and night would be like. (If you don't have a daughter, invent one for this question.) _____

_____

_____

_____

_____

_____

_____

2. Imagine your daughter being forced into prostitution at age 14. What are some ways that the pimp would use to "break" her to make her obey and to make her pretend she enjoys it? _____

_____

_____

_____

_____

_____

_____

3. Darlene's story is very typical of how women end up as prostitutes. Most women don't choose it as a career. Most women who pose for porn have the same story. They smile for the camera but were lured in or forced in by men. List the excuses that you may have used to justify visiting a prostitute or looking at porn. _____

_____

_____

_____

_____

_____

_____

_____

_____

# Not for Sale

You heard a voice cry out,

Look the other way.

I'm not a face you see.

Another stranger calls.

I am not the name they see.

I am not a human being.

Caged by modern desire,

I am just a piece of fuel

Stoking their raging fire.

Creature of the night,

I wasn't meant to be

Used, confused, abused,

By those that surround me.

I never had a voice;

I never had a choice.

I am a modern slave.

When morning comes it is bright.

I've been out all night.

I want my freedom;

I want my life.

I'm here in chains, a modern-day slave.

My love is not for sale.[95]

# DEALING WITH TERROR: SHOULD A CHILD EVEN HAVE TO?

by Lachelle

When I was a child I was violated by someone I trusted. This person looked so good from the outside that no one ever suspected him; and no one would believe me either. Yet I was sexually abused.

Now, as a grown woman, I try to live a holy life and keep a loving attitude, yet inside I am forced to face the shame that overwhelms me because of abuse – the desires of my abuser's heart were played out upon *me* when I was a child.

Children who have been sexually abused often experience a level of fear that is difficult to even describe. These feelings can go *way* beyond fear. They have been called "indescribable." The closest wording I can come up with is *"debilitating terror"*.

I was four years old when my traumatic events started. I am now an adult, yet at times I have dealt with feelings of such terror that I can barely walk out of the house, let alone be with people.

My abuser personally came to violate me at a young age while I was sound asleep. As a result, sleeping as an adult became a disturbing event. *Will the abuse ever be repeated?* I often wondered. *Is it safe for me to close my eyes?* Every rustle or noise made me alert. *There could be trouble again.* Terror stalked me at night. *Perhaps I shall stay awake all night watching . . . . ?*

These are the awful results on the other side of an addict's desire. This is the human perspective that men who sexually harm others may not have considered. We who were mistreated are not toys or lifeless objects; we are human. We are children, young women, and often young men. We were helpless and dependent on the very adults that harmed us.

**Reflections:**

Dear reader, if this applies to you, perhaps these words will enter your heart. Perhaps, thinking about what Lachelle has said will keep just one child from ever being harmed, or from being harmed again. That is one goal of this book.

1. What feelings arise in your heart and thoughts in your mind as you read this story? _____
   _____
   _____
   _____
   _____

   What are some healthy ways of dealing with these feelings and thoughts?
   _____
   _____
   _____
   _____
   _____

2. We who were abused are humans, not toys. Is it possible to value a woman or child and still hurt them? _____
   _____
   _____
   _____

3. Have you ever wounded anyone who was helpless? _____
   _____
   _____
   _____

# LETTER FROM A WOMAN:
## TO THE MAN WHO INJURED ME

As a child I looked up to you, and sought out your approval and acceptance. I wanted nothing more than to love you and to be loved by you. I wanted to be held in your arms and feel the comfort of your protectiveness. For more than thirteen years you treated me the way I needed to be treated, and I felt loved. In return I gave you all the unconditional love I could give.

Apparently my unconditional love was not enough. You wanted more than a child was expected to give. You touched me in places that were inappropriate. Your heart and mind must have enjoyed what your hands touched, because you touched me there so many times.

To this day I am unable to handle the physical touch of another human being. I cringe each time I experience any physical contact.

Because of this anxiety I am unable to lower my guard and trust another to let them get close. Because of what happened, I have spent seventeen years alone.

I have often felt like giving up. Those hands, fingers, and lips haven't only molested my once young body, but they molested my heart, mind, and life.

To this day I have tried my best to forget the feelings of those hands, fingers, and lips on my body. I have tried to forget the scent of liquor which you so often breathed on me, and how it was often used as an excuse for this behavior.

Why do we need to talk about such difficult stories? My intent in this section from women is to bring these difficult issues into the light and point the way toward genuine and sincere confession, transformation, and freedom. The pain in this letter reveals to us the incredible damage caused by the person who injured her.

**Reflections:**

1. Sometime it is almost unbearable to admit the pain that our actions have caused those whom we love.

   If you are not yet willing to "see" the extent of pain that your actions have caused, will you ask God to help you become willing to see?

   _____

   This is an important step for your healing.

2. What did God tell you? _____
   _____
   _____
   _____
   _____
   _____
   _____
   _____

# IN THE SHADOWS[97]

They say: that if it feels good, why not do it.
They say: it doesn't hurt anyone.
They say: they have the right to do what they please.
But crying in the shadows I can see.
If this is love, why does it hurt so bad inside?
Why do moms and children run and hide?
Why is there so much darkness?
Did they tell you a lie?
Why, there in the shadows, do they cry?

The Bible says come out from the darkness,
And do what's holy and pure to the Lord.

And this is love: God sent His Son for us.
And this is love: Jesus gave
His life for me.
He came to shine a light in the darkness,
He came to set the captive free.
He came to shine a light in the darkness,
He came to make the shadows flee.

## At the Heart of "In the Shadows":

The words to "In the Shadows" came from a very tough place in my life. After being asked to paint a sign to advertise a conference on decency (an effort to try to clean up and put restrictions on pornographic material on store shelves back in the late 70s), awareness and some deep heartache began to surface in me. The sign to be painted was a picture of a small girl crouching in a corner of a room, crying with her head down in shame, and afraid, with anguish on her face. As I began to draw and paint the sign, I could feel, and relate to, the image of this broken girl. At the time I was in an abusive marriage; my spouse was addicted to pornography and my children and I were suffering as a result of this damaging behavior. My children and I experienced sexual, mental and physical abuse. We lived in constant fear. I spent many years holding the pain inside, and wanting a healthy happy love-filled home for my children and me. I stayed in the relationship for thirty-eight years and finally divorced and tried to move on. I believe people need to know the effect pornography can have on a family.

The hurt is real, the pain is real....They all need to heal...

# SEVERE SOLUTION:
# DEALING WITH DISSOCIATION

by Betsy

Sometimes sexual abuse can affect a child so deeply that they can develop a form of amnesia called "dissociation" or Dissociative Identity Disorder (DID).[10]

Dissociation is an automatic protection in our brains that allows us to keep living in the midst of severe abuse. It is not a conscious choice; it's something that just happens when traumas reach an overwhelming level.

A victim separates, or dissociates, from an extremely painful event in order to survive emotionally. People (especially children before the age of seven years old) who experience repeated traumas use this as a way to cope with or to endure the unbearable emotional pain of abuse.

Dissociation can be the only way some can cope with what happened to them as a child. Either forget what happened, or "simply go nuts" is the way one survivor put it. I see the mind's ability to dissociate as a gift to prevent insanity, especially in small children.

Sometimes the memories encase, or enclose, themselves. The brain tucks these memories away into "parts" or "alters." These new identities or personalities are split off to carry the painful memories. Each part stores its own memory along with the extreme negative and painful emotions that go with it.

It's hard to believe, but the victim is totally unaware they have parts or different personalities. Maybe you saw the movie *Sybil*, starring Sally Field, about an abuse victim with 16 different personalities.

---

10   For more information on this condition, see: Hawkins, Diane, Multiple Identities: Understanding and Supporting the Severely Abused (Grottoes, VA: Restoration in Christ Ministries, 2009) Used by permission. All rights reserved. *http://www.rcm-usa.org/*

## Dissociation Is Temporary

Eventually, these defense mechanisms need to unravel so that the person can face reality and deal with the past abuse and all the bad effects from it. This often happens when people get *triggered*. Triggers are caused by an event or person that (consciously or unconsciously) reminds the abuse victim of a past event or person. The trigger causes the memory of the original event to come rushing into the person's conscious mind, bringing along all the terror, grief, or other emotions related to that original event. It is awful, and the victim never knows when the trigger will strike or where he will be – which is equally awful.

## Memories Came Flooding Back

Although I had lots of stress and terror in my life, I was unaware of any of my past abuse. My memories started to emerge when my children became the age I was when I was first abused.

I went through a horrible time of actually becoming a child of seven years old again. My husband and I were out walking, and suddenly it seemed that I was looking way up to his face. I had reverted to a child of seven, and he wasn't aware that he was really holding hands with someone who had emotionally changed back to a small child.

This is how I realized that something seriously wrong had happened to me at age seven. Imagine the shock, both to me and to my husband.

These memories were confirmed by another family member who started remembering the abuse as well. The deeds became uncovered. My whole life was interrupted, as was the life of my family.

Many times memories came separately from each other. I received several pictures of the abuse over a period of time. It was confusing, to say the least. For this season I could barely function, let alone be a wife and take care of my children.

One time I was driving down the street from my own home and actually got lost. I did not know where I was, and I was terrified. It was then that I realized more sexual abuse had occurred. I learned that I was taken by car to another location to be molested, and this abuse came back to my memory.

I could not sleep normally. I would wake up in the middle of night, often in terror. This happened because I was taken to be abused in the dead of night.

My life stood still so I could try to get a grasp on reality and try to get some inner healing and therapy so I could function – not only as a member of society, but as a member of society trying to live a godly life and raise a family.

No one should have to try and live under these conditions. *Do I walk out the door, dreading that I will become a child in the company of adults*, I wondered? It was easier just to stay home.

I tried to hide myself and the painful issues that had taken over my entire life. Trying to seek acceptance from other people usually required that I hide behind an artificial mask. I wondered *Who would want to be friends with someone so broken?* I lived in shame. Yet all these horrific issues did not come at my own choosing. I was an innocent victim.

Dissociative Identity Disorder is a very difficult thing to live through. Abuse has cost me years of my life, thousands of dollars spent on counseling, and it has splintered family relationships. It's been over 50 years since the abuse happened and it's not over yet. I'm still seeing counselors and fighting to try to live a normal life.

**Reflections:**

1. "Parts of you" can come forward and share their stories when they feel safe. When they feel loved they are less afraid to share the events and traumas they have experienced.

   Maybe you are dissociated or maybe not, but a man's dark secrets and hidden sins can safely surface in God's love and in His power. Ask God to help you bring forward your own issues in the presence of His love, and ask Him to help you to turn from them. His loving heart is reaching out for you now.

   Write down what He told you: _____

   _____

   _____

   _____

   _____

   _____

   _____

# THE CONVENIENCE OF ABORTION

by Samantha

Tears are streaming down my face – many, many tears. . . . The sadness I feel inside as I write is more than anyone can even imagine.

My baby, you are lost and now I feel so empty, like a deep hole inside of me refusing to be filled.

I lost my baby to another person's need. It was greed that brought my pimp to remove the one placed inside my womb. While another's pleasure "needed" to be fulfilled, it placed an ache inside of me.

### I Wanted to Die

I still feel a pain in my heart – a pain that will not go away, even after several years of leaving my old life behind. When I was forced to have an abortion, the trauma hit my heart so hard that I wanted to die. I do not say the words "suicidal tendencies" lightly. I know them daily. I struggle to live every day.

Nor do I say the word "depression" in a light manner – that state of unhappiness and hopelessness that was always with me. I would do almost anything to remove the agony, the pain, and the emptiness in my heart – drugs, drinking, whatever. But no matter what I did, there was never enough of it to really dull the pain, or fill the hole within.

How could I live with the shame? I hid within myself, too fearful to let others see me or get close to me.

I have physically washed and washed, trying to remove this filth I feel inside. But there you have it – it is within. It is untouchable by human flesh or by soap and water. The pain, the torment and the sorrow are unbearable. I wonder, how can I go on this way? I keep trying to forgive, but it doesn't come easily. Only the anger and the pain come easily, and then simply remain. My head is held down by the shame, agony, and guilt put upon me. My eyes drop; I want to become invisible. The deeds done against me were a violation of my identity, my body, and my soul.

## Abortion Is Murder

Abortion is murder, a double murder: a loss of life to a should-be new-born baby and a loss within the woman who should have carried and delivered him.

I will always carry the memory of a child who *could have* been and *should have* been. It is like a mental knife stabbing at me, as well as emotional robbery.

People don't want to talk about the horrific traumatic effects of an abortion, but we should talk about these things to drive out the misconceptions and bring the reality needed to change this harmful situation. Abortion hurts women and takes the lives of beautiful babies.

Abortion is devastating to the very heartbeat of the human family. It has become socially acceptable murder.

### Reflections:

1. What do you think of the comment that abortion is "socially acceptable murder"? _____

   _____

   _____

   _____

   _____

2. As a father, have you ever lost a child through abortion? _____

   _____

Society has told us it's "not a child", but that's not true. This daughter or son would have adored you and called you "Daddy". Take some time to realize this loss. If you really get in touch with this, you may need to speak to a trusted friend or a counselor. Women aren't the only ones who grieve after abortions. This is a serious loss for a man also.

# WHAT IS THIS "THING" CALLED LOVE, ANYWAY?

by Jackie

### What's love got to do with it?[98]

Tina Turner recorded a song in 1984 called *What's Love Got to Do with It?* Some of her lyrics are as follows:

> Oh, what's love got to do, got to do with it,
> What's love but a second-hand emotion;
> What's love got to do, got to do with it,
> Who needs a heart
> When a heart can be broken?

John Lennon of the Beatles told us just the opposite: "Love is all you need."[100] He's right. It has everything to do with it, if "it" (quoted from Tina Turner above) means having a meaningful life.

But what *is* love?

Again, from Tina Turner's song:

> It's physical
> Only logical
> You must try to ignore
> That it means more than that.

If love is only physical and logical, then we are left in a sad situation.

### Two Views of Love

For many song writers, poets, and movie producers, love is all about doing our own thing; it's about marching to our own drum. It is ultimately self-centered. It's all about *me* and rarely about the other. It's been said that "Men use love to get sex; women use sex to get love." Women give sex to men hoping the men will fall in love with them, and men treat women kindly hoping to get sex. How sad to manipulate a person for your own personal gain.

Fulfilling our own impulses and getting our own basic needs met is called *eros love* and it is named after the Greek god of erotic love. *Eros* love is all about fulfilling our own impulses and gratifying our own basic needs. This is not the highest form of love. *Eros* love is not satisfying to your soul, nor is it nurturing to the receiver. Technically, it probably shouldn't even be called love.

Yet love – true love – actually is all we need. It's called *agape love* and it's selfless – the very opposite of *eros*. Real, true, authentic love is found in laying down our lives for our friends[11] -- and even for our enemies.

The following true story is an amazing example of *agape* love:

> A woman's only son was killed. She was consumed with grief and hatred and bitterness. "God," she prayed, "reveal my son's killer." One night she dreamed she was going to heaven. But there was a complication: in order to get to heaven, she had to pass through a certain house. She had to walk down the street, enter the house through the front door, go through its rooms, up the stairs, and exit through the back door. She asked God whose house this was. "It's the house," He told her, "of your son's killer." The road to heaven passed through the house of her enemy. Two nights later, there was a knock at her door. She opened it, and there stood a young man. He was about her son's age. "Yes?" He hesitated. Then he said, "I am the one who killed your son. Since that day, I have had no life. No peace. So here I am. I am placing my life in your hands. Kill me. I am dead already. Throw me in jail. I am in prison already. Torture me. I am in torment already. Do with me as you wish." The woman had prayed for this day. Now it had arrived, and she didn't know what to do. She found, to her own surprise, that she did not want to kill him. Or throw him in jail. Or torture him. In that moment of reckoning, she found she only wanted one thing: a son. "I ask this of you. Come into my home and live with me. Eat the food I would have prepared for my son. Wear the clothes I would have made for my son. Become the son I lost." And so he

---

11   Greater love has no one than this: to lay down one's life for one's friends. John 15:13.

did. Followers of Jesus do what God himself has done, making sons and daughters out of bitter enemies, feeding and clothing them, blazing a trail to heaven straight through their houses. She was acting just like her Heavenly Father. She was making peace. And through her, God's kingdom was expressed.[101]

Agape love is considered the greatest of all virtues, qualities, or assets we can ever hope to achieve.[12]

### But Where, Oh Where, Is the Source?

Imperfect human love will always fall short. The source of this true love is divine; it comes from the Father, through His Son, Jesus. When Jesus was on earth, His motivation was to display the Father's love. Jesus wanted to pass His Father's love to everyone.

God's love is limitless. It is so perfect that the human mind can't even understand it. God is *the* source of true and authentic love. When God enters a relationship with us through His Son, Jesus Christ, He promises vows of permanence, unfailing love, right relationship, fair treatment, tenderness, security, continuing self-revelation, and an eternity together in Heaven. His love is not based on emotions or on whether we are good enough. He relates with His people in loving–kindness. He is aware of their needs (He is focused on other people, not Himself) and has compassion upon us as His very own children.

Here is one woman's struggle to find agape love:

> I was swept up in a world of Eros. I worked in an industry filled with sex and lust. I was a star entertainer in the world of pornography. Driven by money and then later drugs, I sold myself over and over again to find this love: someone to shelter me, to make me feel clean, to make me believe in me. It was never found in Eros. I didn't find it as a magazine centerfold. I didn't find it in a stadium of screaming, adoring fans. I didn't find it in the sexual partners I chose. I found it at the very bottom of my life on the floor, in a simple prayer. I asked God for this agape love. I asked Him to forgive me, and I accepted the sacrifice of His Son, Jesus. Today, I walk in a love that I could have only imagined. Real. Unconditional. Agape.[102]

---

12   "And now these three remain: faith, hope and love. But the greatest of these is love" (1 Corinthians 13:13).

The Lord is our source of agape love, and we receive love from Him. Then, and only then, can we share it with other people. We cannot give away what we do not already have. Once we have received this love ourselves, it shows in our actions, not just our words.

We connect with this source of life and love as we draw near to Him in prayer, as we study the Bible and quite often in worship and praise. Worship actually draws Him near, like a magnet draws itself to metal. It can feel like the true and living God is bending way down from Heaven to draw near to you, to just be close.

God's love is also found through His followers in church (although no person on earth can display God's love perfectly as we are all growing in His love). Christ is head of the church, and His love flows through us to one another. Small groups within the church can be a perfect example of this other-centered love. People care for each other by making phone calls to find out how someone is doing, by praying for one another, and through simple acts of kindness. These are all demonstrations of His love:

> We know what real love is because Jesus gave up His life for us. So we also ought to give up our lives for our brothers and sisters. If someone has enough money to live well and sees a brother or sister in need but shows no compassion— how can God's love be in that person? Dear children, let's not merely say that we love each other; let us show the truth by our actions (I John 3:16-18, NLT).

Try to wake up each morning thinking of a person you can be kind to. Be kind each day by focusing on helping and serving others instead of yourself. When we do this, we become a channel of God's love, and we live a successful life that pleases Him and blesses others.

> **You can't always do great things but you can always do small things with great love.[103]**

When you love people in God's way instead of the eros way, you will be surprised to find it is very satisfying. It is opposite of the way most people think and act. Trust that when God says it is greater to give than it is to receive,[13] He is right!

---

13    "In everything I did, I showed you that by this kind of hard work we must help the weak, remembering the words the Lord Jesus Himself said: 'It is more blessed to give than to receive.' " Acts 20:35.

Even if you refuse to live for Jesus, nothing can separate you from His love. He loves even the most self-centered and ungodly people. His love alone is not a ticket into Heaven because His love will not forgive unrepented sin for which one has not asked forgiveness, and from which one has not turned away. His love gives you the opportunity to accept Him as your Savior, Lord, and Friend –- and it can start you on a brand new way of life.

**Reflections:**

1. Have you ever been hurt so badly that you thought, " *Who needs a heart when a heart can be broken?"* _____
   _____
   _____

2. Thankfully, most of us will not have to forgive someone who murdered our son. But who is it that you hate the most right now? _____
   _____
   _____
   _____
   _____
   _____

3. Knowing that they don't deserve forgiveness, can you ask the Lord to help you give it to them anyway? _____
   _____
   _____
   _____
   _____
   _____

4. Has your relationship with the opposite sex been mostly about giving or mostly about getting? _____
   _____
   _____
   _____
   _____
   _____

# DEBBIE – A SPOUSE'S PERSPECTIVE

(Debbie is married to Bill Corum who wrote chapter 1:
Pornography – My Drug of Choice)

I was 26 and Bill was 35 when we met in September of 1979. He had been divorced four years. I had been separated from my first husband for seven months but was not yet divorced. Bill and I started living together in January 1980 and married a few months later.

At that time, I relied heavily upon alcohol to keep raging anxiety attacks at bay and to function each day. Bill was an alcoholic who did drugs. When alcohol abuse threatened to destroy our fragile relationship, we agreed to quit in order to save our marriage.

I followed through. He didn't. But by eliminating the alcohol crutch from my life, the anxiety monster was unleashed again, and this time worse than ever. A psychiatrist prescribed Thorazine, and my dad gave me Valium. Bill, who had become a full-blown drug dealer by then, introduced me to Quaaludes as his solution. Over time, Quaaludes became my drug of choice.

As Bill's pornography addiction came into clearer view, the more perverted and distant our relationship grew. Pornography couldn't help but affect our intimacy. Bill wanted to experiment with new ways of coming together –and he introduced me to a world of perversion I never knew existed.

This was my second marriage, and both husbands were unfaithful. Both found sexual satisfaction elsewhere. Because of that, I tried as best I could to do whatever it took to make Bill happy, to make him desire me, to keep him home and satisfied with me.

But in trying to keep him content, I found myself giving in to pretended sexual satisfaction and sinking deeper and deeper into shame, anger, worthlessness, self-hatred, and despair. My sense of low and often *no* self-worth made me angry. I was angry at myself for giving in to such loose morals when I knew better. I was angry because I couldn't figure out *what* I needed to change about myself to make things different, or *how* to change me. I was angry at Bill for not loving me and for using me in his thirst for gratification. After all, I deserved better didn't I?

The shame message played loud and clear in my mind, and I embraced it and made it my own. *Debbie, you are deficient. You don't have what it takes to keep a man. This is the second husband you've lost. There's something wrong with you; you need to change. You need to be someone else, do something more, do it better. You are the problem.* I was ashamed of who I was. I was ashamed of my habit of picking unfaithful men who devalued me.

Twice during that period of time, I battled sexually transmitted diseases. One condition took four different doctors and six months to determine the diagnosis and successfully treat. This added to my sense of shame.

Surrendering my life to Jesus Christ in December 1981 marked the beginning of my climb out of that deep hole I found myself in. Jesus delivered me from anxiety attacks instantly. My addiction to drugs also ended.

The deliverance from perversion and the healing I desperately needed was a slow process because of my husband's pornography addiction. My deliverance began with a revelation of Jesus' love for me, and that revelation transformed me. Little by little, He brought me *out of* the old Debbie I'd known and the standards by which I measured her . . . *by bringing me into* my new identity I found my self-worth in Him.

I began referring to myself as the Isaiah 54 woman:

> "For your Maker is your husband—the Lord Almighty is
> His name—the Holy One of Israel is your Redeemer; He is
> called the God of all the earth. The Lord will call you back
> as if you were a wife deserted and distressed in spirit—a
> wife who married young, only to be rejected," says your
> God (Isaiah 54:5-6).

Like her, I was wooed and won in my youth, only to later be refused and scorned by my husband—or in my case, two husbands. I discovered the wonders of experiencing my Maker as my new Husband, instead of Bill.

I gained courage when I read His promises in Isaiah 54:1-3 that my insignificant, unfruitful life was going to bust loose and get bigger than I ever imagined now that I had Christ. I would actually forget the shame of my youth and not remember the disgrace of my widowhood any more.

> "Sing, barren woman, you who never bore a child; burst into song, shout for joy, you who were never in labor; because more are the children of the desolate woman than of her who has a husband," says the Lord. "Enlarge the place of your tent, stretch your tent curtains wide, do not hold back; lengthen your cords, strengthen your stakes. For you will spread out to the right and to the left; your descendants will dispossess nations and settle in their desolate cities."

> "Do not be afraid; you will not be put to shame. Do not fear disgrace; you will not be humiliated. You will forget the shame of your youth and remember no more the reproach of your widowhood. (Isaiah 54:1-4)

Jesus, my wonderful new Husband placed great value on me, in a way that Bill couldn't. My new Husband took great care of me and provided for me. His Word became so alive when I read it; that there were times I thought I might explode. I'll never forget one night when Bill had been gone for weeks. Jesus held me and comforted me in my abandonment and extreme loneliness.

I know now that God gave me a gift of faith for that extremely difficult season. Otherwise, I never would have made it. I was convinced that since He drew me into salvation, (forgiven of sin and given eternal life as a gift) He would draw my husband, as well. I would wait.

But my increasing faith and those changes in me brought additional problems in our sexual relationship. It became more and more difficult to comply with my husband's perverted desires. As I set personal boundaries of what I would submit to sexually, the strain between us increased. I found myself caught between my old broken ways and what I read in the Scriptures. I agonized over what God's Word meant for me and how I was to love and honor my husband until Jesus got hold of him.

I prayed much over Scriptures like:

> 1 Corinthians 7:13-14 (KJV) "And the woman which hath a husband that believeth not, and if he be pleased to dwell

with her, *let her not leave him. For the unbelieving husband is sanctified by the wife. . ."* (Italics mine).

1 Corinthians 7:34 (NLT) "In the same way, a woman who is no longer married or has never been married can be devoted to the Lord and holy in body and in spirit. *But a married woman has to think about her earthly responsibilities and how to please her husband"* (Italics mine).

Ephesians 5:33 (Amp.) "And the wife see that she *respects and reverences her husband* (that she notices him, regards him, honors him, prefers him, venerates, and esteems him; and that she defers to him, praises him, and loves and admires him exceedingly.)" (Italics mine)

Hebrews 13:4 (NASB) "Marriage is to be held in honor among all, and *the marriage bed is to be undefiled . . ."* (Italics mine.)

Bill started staying away more and more. Sometimes he would disappear for weeks at a time, until April 1983. The day he surrendered his life to Jesus, the perversion ended and the healing began with both of us in full agreement.

The healing of our marriage has been a process of leaving the old and coming into the wonderful new—both in our identities in Christ and in how we treat each other. It's been a journey of love, forgiveness, and much healing. Is our healing complete? That's God's decision. But when a wife, whose first husband dubbed her a 'dead fish' in bed, comes together with a former perverted sex maniac and both are satisfied with each other, that is progress for sure!

We've been married 34 years. The last 31 have been good, with the Lord at the center. We give Him the glory!

Here's my advice to any woman living in a similar circumstance:

Healing begins with a personal relationship with Jesus Christ. As you come to know Him, you will come to know who you are and your true worth. There is no other way.

I haven't done everything right in my journey into healing and wholeness. I've made many mistakes along the way. But I am loved by God. And because I'm forgiven by His blood that He shed on the cross, I am viewed by God as blameless and holy. I am following Him as His disciple. That's what

He's asked of me. I'm at peace.

Your journey into healing and wholeness will look different than mine because you are unique in Him. As long as you keep moving ahead with Jesus and keep seeking more of Him, you'll do fine. Don't stay stuck in the muck. He will bring you out of the old bondage and into your unique destiny in Him.

**Reflections:**

1. "As you come to know Him, you will come to know who you are and come to understand your true value. There is no other way. Little by little, He brought me *out of* the old Debbie I'd known." Here is what the Bible says about who you are. Read and pray over these scriptures, asking God to help you believe the truth.

   In Christ:

   - I am loved: 1John 3:3
   - I am accepted: Ephesians 1:6
   - I am a child of God: John 1:12
   - I am redeemed and forgiven: Colossians 1:14
   - I am free from condemnation: Romans 8:1
   - I am a new creation because I am in Christ: 2Corinthians 5:17
   - I am chosen of God, holy and dearly loved: Colossians 3:12
   - I do not have a spirit of fear, but of love, power, and a sound mind: 2Timothy 1:7

   I have direct access to God, through Jesus Christ: Ephesians 2:18
   I can ask God for wisdom and He will give me what I need: James 1:5

   Simply **choose** to believe what God says about you, if you are a born again believer in Christ (forgiven of sin and given eternal life as a gift.). Which one will you start with? _____
   _____
   _____
   _____
   _____

Before you start. . .

## AN OPEN LETTER TO
## CHILD SEXUAL ABUSERS

The following letter was written by a sexual abuse survivor who was struck by the enormous difference in the amount of time that it takes for someone to sexually abuse a child and the time that the child will have to bear its effects.

*Do these people really know the effect that their momentary desire for pleasure will have on their victims?* She wondered. *Would it make any difference to them if they did?*

For whatever chance there might be to help prevent future harm, she decided she could not remain silent. She had to do what she could to cry out in the hope that it would help to make a difference and spare even a few others from carrying the lifelong scars she herself bears.

By writing this letter, she would also become a voice for many, many other victims whose silent pain needs to be heard. Please consider deeply what she has to say.

Dear Father, Stepfather, Grandfather, Brother, Uncle, Babysitter, Neighbor, Priest, whoever you are –

You who see that innocent child playing happily in her yard, lying peacefully in her bed – you who are tempted to suavely enter her private domain and take a little sexual joy for yourself, my heart cries to you from its deepest depths, "BEFORE YOU TOUCH, please, PLEASE, PLEASE, oh please, consider what damage you are inflicting upon her.

"Just one time," you say.

"She won't be aware; she's sleeping."

"She's too young to even know it's wrong."

"She'll think we're playing."

"I won't go all the way."

"She needs to learn about sex."

Yes, you have your excuses, your reasons, and your alibis; but deep down you know that it's your own self-centered pleasure and the need to feel your power that lies at the heart of this lustful desire. Oh, selfish man, will you not realize that the power of love and self-control is by far the mightier sword to wield? It leaves no scars of guilt or shame or remorse – no scars on you and no scars on her. Scars are forever, my friend. The wounds may heal, but the scars never ever completely disappear. Do you really want to wound her? Do you really want her to bear the permanent scars of your selfish pleasure? What has she done, I ask you, what has she done to deserve such a destiny?

---

*SOME OF THE CONSEQUENCES OF ABUSE*
*IN MEN AND WOMEN INCLUDE:*
*Raging fear – from past events and fear of further abuse,*
*The inability to feel comfortable around people,*
*Haunting by images of abuse when your eyes are closed,*
*Emotional shattering,*
*Predisposition to alcoholism and drug abuse,*
*Hostility, depression, psychosomatic illnesses,*
*either promiscuity or frigidity.*

"You talk of wounds and scars and destiny," I hear you say. "I'm talking of only a touch, only a caress, only a feel. I do not mean to damage her."

And that is just why I am writing to you. You do not know the depth of agony that touch, that caress, that feel will cause that child to bear. The fact that she has been betrayed by one in whom she fearlessly put her love and trust will be too overwhelming for her to handle as a child.

The reaction you see will be small or even one of positive receptivity as she drinks in the feeling of pseudo-affection for which she has perhaps been starved, but don't you know that down the road, yes, down the road someday she will have to deal with this memory of violation and abuse? Sooner or later she will know that those were hands that moved not in love for her, not in warm affection, but only for themselves. They took; they did not give. They took that which was most precious to her, that which was to be hers alone.

And then the pain – the searing, tearing, tormenting pain – will wrench the very depths of her being: the pain of betrayal, the pain of humiliation and shame, the pain of being used instead of loved, exploited instead of protected. And that pain won't last just a day, nor just a week. It will go on for months and months and perhaps even years as she resurrects those long-buried emotions which she could never express as a child, those emotions that subtly continue to hold her life in dismal bondage. They will all need to come out in order for her ever to be set free from their power.

It will take much strength and courage on her part to walk the long, fiery road to healing. But if she doesn't, she will continue to be plagued by deep inner hostility, depression, psychosomatic illnesses, and malfunctions in many areas of her life. It will undoubtedly affect her ability to relate to men in a healthy way. She will be caught between the extremes of fear and sexual frigidity, on the one hand, and promiscuity on the other, knowing how to relate to men only through sex, forever craving the true love and affection she never got as a child. She will have difficulty in forming deep, trusting relationships. Her enormous load of repressed anger will unexpectedly explode at inappropriate times and usually at those she loves the most.

If she has children, she may be hindered in developing the normal intimacy of the parent-child relationship. She may even be inclined to mistreat them, thus continuing the cycle of abuse. In any case, the joy of motherhood will probably be much decreased for her as she battles feelings of inadequacy, guilt, self-hate, and depression. She will also be greatly predisposed to alcoholism and drug abuse, unconsciously trying to escape from the inner pain which haunts her so relentlessly.

These, my friend, are just a few of the damages she will suffer from your selfish act. Do you really want her to be marred in this way? Please, I beg you again; please consider these facts – BEFORE YOU TOUCH.

Painfully written by . . .
Restoration in Christ Ministries[104]

**Reflections:**

1. Circle any excuses you have heard from others, thought about using, or used yourself:

    "Just one time."

    "She won't be aware; she's sleeping."

    "She's too young to even know it's wrong."

    "She'll think we're playing."

    "I won't go all the way."

    "She needs to learn about sex."

    "I'm talking of only a touch, only a caress, only a feel. I do not mean to damage her."

2. List three effects identified in the article above that sexual abuse has on a child:

    a. _____

    b. _____

    c. _____

3. What is the main thing you learned from this article? _____

_____

_____

4. What will you do with what you learned? _____

_____

_____

Read Elaine's amazing story of faith, grace, forgiveness, and love. See the heart of God expressed in ways that are truly remarkable. Elaine is the wife of Jonathon Daugherty, who wrote Seven Strategies for Strugglers (pg 83).

# ELAINE'S STORY

by Elaine Daugherty

Once upon a time there was a little girl that believed in happy ever after...

That little girl was me. Jonathan and I got married in the winter of 1995. It felt like the beginning of a fairy tale, and of course every girl dreams of "happy ever after" following her wedding day. Boy, was I in for some surprises. What I did not know at the time was what the Lord would use to teach us, or that we would see more wicked witches, gremlins, and places like hell than we would first see of "happy ever after."

One evening after we had been married several months, Jonathan came to me with something in his hand. He was ashamed and downcast. He held a department store magazine out in his hand and he told me that he had looked at the pictures of the women and masturbated. It was not a Playboy or anything that graphic; it was just a department store magazine with some scantily clad women in it. I really felt hurt. I looked at the women and thought that they were much skinnier than I was, much prettier... I thought I had not met his needs as a new bride and that is what sent him to imagine things with other women.

That was my first exposure that Jonathan had a problem with pornography, but I was young and so naïve. I had no clue how serious a problem it was or how deeply involved he was. I told myself that he was so godly to have confessed his sins on his own without being caught. I thought of what worse magazines he could have looked at and was glad that things were not as bad as they could have been. When he asked my forgiveness that day, I gave it and easily washed the smudge of dirt from my knight's armor.

I secretly determined to lose some weight and be more available to him sexually.

The issue of pornography did not surface again for a while, yet our marriage was going through a rough time and, looking back, porn was the driving force.

I thought things were normal even though my heart longed for more.

Finances became a huge area of strife at that time. We were both finishing school so, naturally, money was tight. But it was more than that... we were headed in different directions. One day I opened the door to our apartment and there was a computer. Jonathan said he had used the credit card. Two thousand dollars in debt (an amount that I thought at the time was monumental, because that was my first experience with the credit card) and a computer; both things were signs of more trouble to come. Credit cards and the computer proved to be thorns in my side. No, not thorns, more like lances. Debt began to pile up. Our $2,000 debt grew to an impossible $20,000. Eventually Jonathan filed for bankruptcy.

Jonathan would come home from work and drown himself on the computer. All I wanted was to spend time with him... so I became kind of a nag about it, which certainly did not aid to our togetherness. I was so selfishly wrapped up in not having my needs met that I did not see my husband sinking in quick sand.

I teasingly (well, half teasingly) called his computer *Jezebel*...it in fact was.[105] The truth about the computer I would find out later. Our moments together usually ended in tense situations or hurt feelings. We often would put on our "happy face" when others were around. I watched my husband pull away, and I grabbed more desperately for him. He may have needed space, but the more I reached for him, the more he felt like a trapped bird. In time he withdrew even more from me.

One summer day in 1997, Jonathan packed his car with all his belongings and took off for Nashville. He left me as a clueless and devastated girl. I had no idea why he left or if he was coming back. What had I done? Was I so hard to live with? These are the thoughts that ran through my mind. I determined that if he ever came back I would keep the house cleaner, cook better, not nag him about spending time with me, lose weight, etc. I had so many plans...

I was embarrassed when people found out about us, because you see, I wanted people to think that I had a perfect marriage. Nineteen days went by until Jonathan returned. He returned apologetic and filled with promises of how much better our marriage would be.

They were short-lived promises, and more dirt in our marriage began to surface. The nameless horrors that plagued our marriage began to have a name. This whole time I had not known that Jonathan was a sex addict, but I began to find it out. He once again admitted his problem to me, and I began to find out all kinds of hidden things. Naughty sites on the Internet would pop up when I turned on the computer, or when I would look in the history file. I became a suspicious, anxious, accusing spy. I found emails, chat sites, and phone numbers. Little by little the truth became clear.

But we were still living under illusions. Promises were constantly made. I enabled him to continue living his secret lives without boundaries in our relationship. I cared too much about what people would think if they knew the truth. I had so much pride. I wanted so badly for the "happy ever after" that I let the hell that was going on continue. I chose to think that things would get better if I just did this or that. The whole while my husband was being drawn further and further in to his sexual addiction.

In August of 1999, I found out that my husband had been physically unfaithful multiple times. I was utterly broken. Every night I prayed that I would die in my sleep because it hurt so badly. Every morning I was astounded that the world went on with life, because I was so hurt that I did not see how life could go on. And yet, every morning, the sun came up. Every day, birds continued to sing, the stars and moon came out in the evening. I was shocked. The song by the Beatles that goes "Ob-la-di, Ob-la-da, life goes on" was true.

We were sleeping in different rooms because I had not left yet. I thought that since he was the one that told me about his infidelities, that he was on the road to recovery and I had been brought up to stay in a marriage, ...to forgive. That week could be described as nothing else but hell. By the end of the week I found out that his behavior was not changing and was continuing, so I packed my things and left. I went to my parents' house. At the time I had no intention of getting back together with Jonathan. I never wanted to see him again; I never even wanted to talk with him. I was at rock bottom. My heart was in millions of pieces.

Little did I know that my leaving that day would be used as a catalyst in Jonathan's life. He had also finally reached rock bottom. He too was broken. God showed me a clear image of the shame that Jonathan had lived with.

At that time, Jonathan even wondered if God could still love him. He was filled with shame.

God began doing amazing things in my husband's life. My husband was broken, totally repentant, and crying out to God. God changed him. Every day while we were separated, I received a letter in the mail from Jonathan. I watched him become a totally different person. I watched him put up safe boundaries in his life. I watched him give up the TV and for over 2 years he gave up the Internet at home and even now that we have it again, it is protected Internet service (SafeEyes). I watched him lay himself vulnerable to people in the church and to an accountability group. Every week, he now meets with other men whom he holds accountable and who hold him accountable. He is living for purity. Every day I watch him start his day with a quiet time with the Lord. I watched him start to love me.

God also changed me. He created a new compassion for Jonathan in my heart. He showed me my own faults and my own unfaithfulness to Him. He helped me discover anew His own forgiveness to me. He created a desire in my heart to forgive Jonathan. God did it for me.

On April 8, 2000 I went back to that big white church where we had originally been married and met the new, changed man. Jonathan and I restated our vows and moved back in together. Jonathan has become the husband I had always dreamed about. And God has heaped blessings on us. He gave us three precious children and I am watching Jonathan become an excellent, awesome father to them. Jonathan lives for purity. He maintains his accountability group, keeps the protective hedges in his life, and daily draws nearer to the Savior. We spent months rebuilding trust and will continue to do so. But I am so happy now. Our life together now is filled with many happy moments. There is hope!

If God can heal our broken marriage, He can help you too.

**Reflection:**

1. Elaine initially blamed herself for her husband's sexual addiction. Was she correct in doing so? _____

   Why or why not? _____

   _____

   _____

2. Elaine made a plan of how to be a better wife to Jonathan. What boundaries could she have put in place, instead? _____

   _____

   _____

3. Every woman wants to please her man. Elaine uses the following phrases to describe the effect of Jonathan's previous addiction on her:

   "Nameless horrors"

   "I was utterly broken. Every night I prayed that I would die in my sleep because it hurt so badly."

   "That week could be described as nothing else but hell."

   "I was at rock bottom. My heart was in millions of pieces."

   Memorize one of these phrases. Write it here: _____

   _____

   Make a commitment to think of the effect that your actions would have on the woman in your life – before you pick up the magazine, turn on the computer, etc.

   Signed: _____

   Dated: _____

You might be wondering what a chapter directed toward wives is doing in this book. Many wives of sexual addicts, in an effort to understand and to help their husbands, read books directed toward men. Darrell Brazil, who wrote the chapters *You Saw Who at the Strip Club?* and *Breaking Point* for this book, has some excellent advice.

## TO MEN AND WOMEN: WHAT EVERY WIFE NEEDS TO KNOW ABOUT A MAN'S STRUGGLE FOR SEXUAL INTEGRITY

by Darrell Brazell

Through my own recovery journey, counseling with couples in crisis and through seeing the damage my addiction did to my lovely wife, I believe that someone needs to advocate for the wives who are often the forgotten victims of pornography.

> *A husband's struggle with pornography and sexual addiction does great damage and I have seen that damage first hand in my wife's eyes.*

A husband's struggle with pornography and sexual addiction does great damage and I have seen that damage first hand in my wife's eyes and in the eyes of many other women. So I want to share some things that have been very helpful to the wives I have counseled over the past eight years.

1. You are not alone! The sad reality is that pornography, masturbation and sexual struggles are at epidemic proportions. At a March 2007 summit of 2000 Christian men, 70% of the audience admitted they were struggling with porn addiction.[106]

I am thoroughly convinced that one of Satan's primary strategies in all our struggles is to keep us silent and keep us isolated. If you are reading this and think you are alone, please ask God to show you individuals with whom you can safely share your story.

2. You are not crazy. Doubts, suspicions and questions are not evidence of insanity or paranoia. Many husbands, peers, and well-meaning pastors, tell wives that they are just being paranoid or that it is not a big deal or other ridiculous things. It is a huge issue.

It is a betrayal that cuts to the very core of the feminine heart. Men justify their actions, yet in Matthew 5:28 Jesus said "I tell you that anyone who looks at a woman lustfully has already committed adultery with her in his heart." He doesn't pull any punches because He understands how damaging it is both to the husband and to the wife. The fact that it hurts you deeply to know your husband gets sexual pleasure by looking at and/or fantasizing about other women is not a sign that there is something wrong with you. God made woman with a heart that longs to be cherished by a husband who "forsakes all others."

3. It is not your fault. Let me repeat that again. It is not your fault. He doesn't look at pornography because you aren't pretty enough. (Halle Berry and Christy Brinkley both divorced husbands in part because they were sex addicts). He doesn't look at pornography because you have gained weight, because you have a temper, because you aren't as interested in sex as he is or because you aren't exciting enough in bed.

No, he looks at pornography because he has a problem. I have yet to work with a man whose real issues didn't start in his childhood and 99% of the men I work with were addicted long before they even met their wife.

Pornography and masturbation are primarily an escape and coping strategy and are just as addictive as cocaine. If you discovered your husband had been addicted to cocaine since he was 14 and you married him at 21 would his addiction be your fault? No, of course not, and neither is this.

4. You most likely only see the tip of the iceberg. An addicted man invariably lies to himself, his wife and others about the severity of his struggle. Men came to me who seemed genuinely broken and eager to confess their problem, yet they still held back significant details. This has been true both for the men who have been caught and men who sought help on their own. The sad reality is all addicts lie about their addiction.

No, I'm not saying that because you found something one time, your husband is a sex addict. However, the odds of your having found everything are pretty slim. Your husband could be the exception, but you are not crazy, mean or vindictive for asking the hard questions.

5. You are not powerless. Many wives thought they were trapped and couldn't do anything. You can't fix him, but you can protect yourself and your children from the incredible collateral damage of pornography and sexual addiction.

You need to honestly look at the effect pornography has on the family. The book *Beyond the Bedroom*[107] proves the incredible damage on the children of sex addicts even when they were not aware of the issue until they were out of the house. *The Drug of the New Millennium*[108] paints a dreadful picture of unchecked pornography in the home.

Wives, you are the mother bear and it is a righteous thing when you go to war against sexual immorality in your own home. God does not expect you to submit to your husband on this issue as God outranks him.

So what can you do? First, try to lovingly confront. Many men long for a way out, but they honestly don't know how. I hated my sexual sin. I despised myself. Many men are in that same place. So, please, even though you may be deeply hurt, ask God to empower you to approach him with gentle firmness.

Second, tell him that your heart is breaking over what you know and ask him to take the initiative to find help. Some men will break with just a simple invitation from the woman they really do love. But don't be fooled by crocodile tears. Many men, when confronted, will cry, seem broken and willing to do whatever they need to do. However, many times they think an apology, a prayer and a promise is enough. Don't believe his words. If he says he won't do it again but doesn't get help, believe his behavior. Struggles in the sexual arena don't go away easily. If this has gone on for any amount of time, he cannot get out of it by himself.

Third, take definitive action. If your husband does not respond to a gentle request to get help then protect yourself, your children and the sexual integrity of your home. Many wives believe that is impossible. I've told many women on the phone that the first step to getting help in our ministry is to have a couple's appointment. They say, "He wouldn't come." My standard reply is, "If he objects tell him 'That's your choice but until you make an appointment you may not sleep in my bed, kiss or touch me.'" He may think you are bluffing, but if you hold your ground I will most likely hear from him within 24 hours. If I don't, then you have one more huge reason to suspect the iceberg is even larger than you realize and that you should do whatever you need to do to protect yourself and your children.

6. You cannot fix him. Let go of the belief that it is your responsibility to get him better. You may learn many good things by reading the books he should be reading; however, he has to do it himself.

You need to realize that you can't keep him from acting out. It isn't your job to constantly monitor his Internet use or keep an accounting of his every waking moment. As hard as it is, you are going to have to release him into God's hands and let him learn from both his victories and his failures.

You also can't fix him by making yourself available for him sexually so that he doesn't struggle. This myth has been promoted by many well-meaning people. Many wives believe or are told it is their job to "help" their husbands this way in the mistaken belief that if they don't have the buildup of sexual pressure, they won't act out. First, it can actually be counter-productive for the husband. One of the basic core lies is "I will die or at least have serious physical and psychological damage if I don't have a sexual release every X number of hours." This just is not true and has been proven by many single men throughout the ages. A man must quit believing this lie to truly find freedom from sexual bondage. If his wife rescues him every time he starts hitting the wall, he cannot discover the truth.

Second, asking a wife to use her sexuality as a "methadone" substitute is insensitive, if not cruel. The only way a woman in pain can do this is by shutting down her own heart and this invariably causes great damage. In fact, many wives have faced significant sexual dysfunction, even several years into recovery, which came, at least in part, from feeling used and even prostituted during the recovery process as a result of this thinking. It is essential to recognize that Paul's teaching on a husband or a wife not withholding sexual intimacies was not written in the context of sexual addiction. It isn't your job to make your husband OK through sex and it doesn't work anyway.

Third, you need to understand if your husband is looking at pornography, because of the way the brain works, it is neurologically impossible for him to not bring those images into the bed with you. It only takes 1/3 of one second for a pornographic image to be seared into the mind and those images will pop back up both intentionally and unintentionally until he has significant time and a conscious decision to shut them down. So, if you don't want to share your bedroom experiences with porn stars, don't be intimate with a husband who has been looking at pornography.

It is also essential that you do not attempt to be his "accountability person." It is a devastating role for a wife to play. A man needs other men with whom he can be accountable. Yes, he also needs to be honest with you about his struggles. However, it is much more effective if he first confesses to another man and then to you because when we confess we all need someone who can be a representative of God's grace and mercy. The only way a wife, upon first hearing her husband's sexual sin against her, can do that is by shutting down her own heart, ignoring her pain and basically giving herself an emotional lobotomy.

> ### *Asking a wife to use her sexuality as a "methadone" substitute is insensitive, if not cruel.*

It is natural and right for her to be hurt and even angry at the impact his sin has on her and her children. Yes, she needs to forgive and if she allows Him to, God will lead her on that path. However, before she can truly forgive, she must first grieve her losses.

7. You must seek help for yourself regardless of what he does. The pain of your husband's betrayal cannot be ignored. You need a counselor or someone with the knowledge and skill to help you heal and work through your hurt and anger.

You probably also need help understanding as to why it's so hard for you to set real boundaries and why you have been willing to ignore the signs when you knew in your gut something was wrong.

You might need help understanding why you were drawn to a man with a sexual addiction in the first place. No, I'm not backtracking on what I said about it not being your fault. However, it is critical to understand that pornography, masturbation and sexual addiction are at their core false intimacies. They are counterfeit substitutes for what the mind and heart really crave – genuine joyful connection with others. If your husband had a sexual addiction before you met him then you need to ask God to show you if there are broken things in your background that left you willing to settle for someone whose addiction left him incapable of true and deep connection.

Where do you turn? A professional counselor who has experience with sexual addiction is worth his or her weight in gold. They can help us discover the origins of our dysfunctional ways and help us learn to take our pain to God rather than medicate it. You may also want to join a support group for wives of men with sexual addiction issues.

Again, regardless of what your husband does, you must seek help for yourself. While we have found the best results when husband and wife are both in recovery, we have also seen great strides taken by one partner who dove into the process. Sometimes when one spouse starts getting healthier the other spouse eventually joins the process.

> *Masturbation and sexual addiction are at their core false intimacies. They are counterfeit substitutes for what the mind and heart crave – genuine joyful connection with others.*

Finally, where can you go for good resources? You can go to our website *www.newhope4si.com* for free downloads, as well as other helpful items. We also have a resource list for wives. I would also highly recommend *An Affair of the Mind*,[109] and *Drug of the New Millennium*[110] and *Co-Dependent No More*.[111] If you know your husband is addicted, Dr. Doug Weiss' *Now That I Know What Should I Do* DVD or audio teaching is a wonderful tool. It is available at *www.sexaddict.com*.[112]

Most importantly, let me leave you with the hope of knowing that the apostle Paul promises in Romans 8:28 "that in all things God works for good for those who love him, who have been called according to his purposes." If you are in a painful place, please know that God will not waste your pain or your tears. Regardless of what your husband does or does not do, if you allow Him, God will find a way to use your current situation to draw you closer to him and bring greater redemption and glory to your life.

**Reflections:**

1. "One of Satan's primary strategies in all our struggles is to keep us silent and keep us isolated." Why are silence and isolation so effective in keeping people trapped? _____

   _____

   _____

   _____

   Has it trapped you?_____

   _____

   _____

   _____

2. "God made woman with a heart that longs to be cherished by a husband who "forsakes all others." Why does this betrayal cut to the very core of the feminine heart? _____

   _____

   _____

   _____

   _____

3. When trying to quit an addiction why aren't "an apology, a prayer and a promise enough"? _____

   _____

   _____

   _____

4. List several reasons the author believes that it isn't the wife's responsibility to get her husband better or to rescue him sexually. _____

   _____

   _____

   _____

   _____

# SECTION III

# From Heaven's Eyes

# BEHIND CLOSED DOORS

Does God really see evil? Does He know what happens behind closed doors?

While on vacation on September 11, 2011, I had a dream. I had told the Lord He could speak to me at any time and at any place. He took me up on it. I saw two children tied up and lying on a bed. I wrote it in my daily journal and labeled the dream "Childhood Torture" and dated it. At first I didn't really understand what it meant.

The next morning, I read a newspaper article[113] about a three-year-old boy who was abducted from the second-floor bedroom of his unlocked home after he fell asleep. The day I saw the newspaper was the day he was found. It said not only that the boy was alive but also that he was uninjured. The boy's return was hailed as "a miracle."

I was stunned at the thought that God wanted me to know this boy's story before I found it in the public newspaper. I wondered, *Why was this important for me to know ahead of time?*

Then I realized, God knows people's actions, whether private or public. Nothing we think we do in secret or in the dark will ever escape His eyes.

## Unharmed?

Because I'd just had this vivid dream I was alerted to this boy's story in a way I wouldn't have been before. I had several responses to this event. First, I felt such compassion toward this victim, an innocent little boy kidnapped as he slept in his own bed. The paper said he was "unharmed." I didn't believe that for a second. I thought, *What will happen to that little boy's sleep? Will he sleep fitfully? Will he wake up with repeated nightmares? Will he re-live that emotional and psychological trauma again and again?*

Next, I thought of the serious pain, fear, and confusion this little boy experienced when he was kidnapped, and I thought of all its l-o-n-g-lasting effects on this little person. The results will probably last into manhood, making it hard for him to relax or trust, and making his future relationships difficult.

I was concerned for this child's future. Such a little boy, with no choice of his own. Truly a victim.[14] I also could sense the agony that his parents surely went through.[114]

Finally, I felt anger — real anger at the gross injustice of it all. Then I turned to Psalm 73, where I saw that GOD sees, and then read on to Psalm 94, where I saw God's anger at injustice.

### God Really Sees

Some people think they can get away with what they do in secret.

Psalm 94:5, 7 tells us, *"They crush Your people, LORD, hurting those You claim as your own. 'The LORD isn't looking,' they say, 'and besides, the God of Israel doesn't care.' "* (NLT)

Psalm 73:11 says, *"'What does God know?' they ask. 'Does the Most High even know what's happening?' "* (NLT)

He sees, He knows and He cares deeply about this child, who is precious in His sight.

Psalm 94 says: *"He will punish them for their wickedness and destroy them for their sins; the Lord our God will destroy them."* Psalm 94:23 (GNT).

Scripture shows the love and justice of God toward broken and hurting victims. The Bible shows He knows and cares about their pain. Rarely do people get involved or help or protect the victim. But God doesn't look the other way, as people often do.

### What's Hidden Will Become Known

Again, Psalm 94 says: *"God made our ears — can't he hear? He made our eyes — can't He see? He scolds the nations — won't He punish them? He is the teacher of us all — hasn't He any knowledge? He will punish them for their wickedness and destroy them for their sins; the Lord our God will destroy them."* Psalm 94:9-10, 23 (GNT).

---

14    Rich Buhler defines a victim as "a person who has experienced destruction at the foun-
      dation of who that person is and in a way that has caused significant hindrance in
      the living of life." The key words in that definition are destruction, foundation, and
      hindrance.

Reading that newspaper article after my dream was proof enough for me to completely believe these Scriptures. The Biblical term "He knows" actually means to "make known, know or to certify." Not only does the Lord know about these hidden activities; He will also make them known (if we don't repent of them). Activity that was concealed and hidden will eventually be made public. Our God sees, He takes into account, and it is NOT okay with Him when children are harmed.

Romans 2:16 states, ". . . in the day when God will judge the secrets of men by Jesus Christ. . . ." (NKJV)

Revelation 20:11-13 says:

> *And I saw a great white throne and the One sitting on it. The earth and sky fled from His presence, but they found no place to hide. I saw the dead, both great and small, standing before God's throne. And the books were opened, including the Book of Life. And the dead were judged according to what they had done, as recorded in the books. The sea gave up its dead, and death and the grave gave up their dead. And all were judged according to their deeds* (NLT).

Please note that there is "no place to hide." No one escapes the judgment seat, whether dead or alive.

In Mark 9:43-47 Jesus had strong words to say about how important it is to avoid sin:

> *If your hand causes you to sin, cut it off. It is better to enter heaven with only one hand than to go into the unquenchable fires of hell with two hands. If your foot causes you to sin, cut it off. It is better to enter heaven with only one foot than to be thrown into hell with two feet. And if your eye causes you to sin, gouge it out. It is better to enter the Kingdom of God half blind than to have two eyes and be thrown into hell.*

This verse has confused some people. Jesus doesn't mean for us to literally pluck out an eye or cut off a body part. But He uses this example to show us that it's time for us to get serious – very serious – about our actions.

Jesus says that it is so important to get rid of sin that if your hand, foot or eye is causing you to sin, you would be better off without them. With your hands you can do violence; with your feet you can walk into places where you really shouldn't go; with your eyes you can see what is not yours; and from that comes lust, stealing and envy. Exaggeration? Not at all! Jesus overturns our priorities. How different from the priority scale of this world!

Celebrities go to great lengths to insure various parts of their bodies. The Beatles, Keith Richards and others insured their fingers. Bruce Springsteen's voice was insured for three million dollars.... And probably most of us would regard it as an utter disaster to lose the use of a hand, or an eye. But according to Jesus' scale of priorities, that loss is nothing compared to losing your chance of eternal life. Even a top international footballer at the peak of his powers would be far better off without his right foot and knowing Christ, than fit and well on his way to hell.... So choose Christ! Choose the way of life.[115] He is telling us that entering Heaven is worth any cost. Heaven, the place of life, joy and peace, and Hell, the place of torment, are both real. Please make sure you end up in Heaven, even if it requires making difficult choices.

**Reflections:**

In the case of this story, the godly response in the face of the harm done to a child is to grieve over the perpetrator's sin and the damage done to this child. If you have done something similar by harming anyone, please know the Lord is waiting to help you to change your life and behavior so that you can live without shame and with a dignity you may have never experienced. Your transformed life would please Him, and it would prevent the pain of another broken life. It is not too late, no matter what you've already done. He loves you.

1. If you really believed that God sees everything, how would it change your activities? _____

_____

_____

_____

_____

2. Do you know that He is waiting and wanting to help you? _____

_____

_____

_____

_____

3. Ask Him now to help you in areas of your life that you can't seem to change.

   What did He say? _____

_____

_____

_____

_____

# THE PERSONAL ENCOUNTER

by Joey

I was down on my knees praying before the Lord one day, focusing on the healing of my abusive past, when I had a several encounters with our wonderful Savior.

Jesus had convicted me of a sin I'd committed and I was repenting of it. I was asking for grace to repent because I was desperate to be changed by God. I saw the Lamb of God come into the room and kneel beside me.

While I watched, I saw my sins and pain transferred to the Lamb of God Himself. Then the Lamb turned into Jesus hanging on the cross of Calvary. I saw His bloody, beaten back as He suffered so painfully. I saw His life leaving Him as He hung on that tree.

As I stood below the cross, His blood, His very own blood, dripped upon me and washed me as white as snow. He was forgiving me and setting me free.

Then I spoke out to our Lord Jesus:

> "Thank You for giving me what I don't deserve
> (forgiveness and mercy) and
> Thank You for taking what You don't deserve"
> (my shame and my pain – the
> consequence of my sin).

Normally my response is to run away from God in my sinful behaviors, but I learned that He truly wanted me to come *to* Him in my weakness and shame. He showed me how much He longed to forgive me and help me to change. This was a life-changing encounter for me personally.

> By His wounds,
> I have been set free of mine.

# NO ONE CAN HIDE

by Janette

As I personally reflect on all that I have been through, especially the sexual abuse at others' hands – I have a sense that God is saying, "Janette, these events will be judged." In other words, He will not let these terrible experiences go unpunished. He has seen; He has taken into account. He cares about His children, and watches those who harm them. What a relief this is to me and, I am sure, to the many other victims to know that their cause is not forgotten.

It is not I who will judge those who abused me, most gratefully. It is Jesus, the Righteous Judge who will be reviewing cases and events.[15] The Bible describes the time when Jesus will return to earth as a judge: "So splendidly dressed, advancing, bristling with power" (Isaiah 63:1, The Message). God is coming to judge those who have broken His people. He will bring justice.

Please consider what the Bible says about Jesus' (the Judge's) Second Coming. Perhaps you think of Jesus only as a gentle, meek and mild Savior. Look again at His return to earth. He returns with strength and power – as a Judge, mighty to save. His appearance is like a mighty lion, coming with power, strength, and great determination. He yearns to destroy sin and to remove the pain and suffering of His people. He is like a jealous husband protecting and even avenging harm done to His beloved. This is the One who comes on behalf of the broken, who could even be *you*.

I went to my sexual abuser and asked for help in dealing with the painful offenses done to me – to my body, soul, memory, and emotions. I wanted an apology or, at the very least, an admission of the harm he did to me. Yet I was turned away and pushed aside. *Was I unimportant? Or was the issue of his sexually abusing me too difficult to face,* I wondered? I was angry at his

---

15  Hebrews 4:13 "All things are open and exposed, naked and defenseless to the eyes of Him with whom we have to do (give account)" (AMP).

denial, his sweeping away of facts and pain, so I turned to God for His help.

> "Silence in the face of evil is itself evil:
> God will not hold us guiltless."[116]

I spoke out to Him for justice. "Make Wrong Things Right" I said. As one of His very own (a believer), I sensed not only that I had a right to call out to Him, but also that He wanted me to do this. (I choke back tears over His goodness as I write.)

To my amazement, I saw God respond. I saw Him pouring out judgment, just the perfect amount of righteous and just judgment, upon the one who had harmed me so deeply, left me so traumatized for so very long, and then turned away at my request for his help. Oddly, as I am being slowly healed, the one who harmed me and denied it is slowly deteriorating. How I want him to turn away from his abuse and its devastating effects.

Over time, I saw the one who looked away from my requests for help slowly go blind. He chose not to see me or my pain when I asked for help. But now, his vision is leaving him. I hold no grudge; I have forgiven him. I have placed him in the hands of One who says, "Vengeance[16] is Mine."[17]

I call this "present-time-judgment" because it's given right now, here on earth. I am grateful that sin does not go unnoticed. The sin done to me now has a partial acknowledgment here on earth.

God cares about what we do to one another. Now I understand that He is the One who sees and the One who hears my distress. Not only that, He has taken account of the significant, painful actions done against me. What an awesome truth this is!

> "You may choose to look the other way,
> But you can never say again
> That you did not know."[117]

To those who do turn from the wrong they have done (and I hope that is you), there is healing. To those who don't, there are consequences, even while here on earth. Matthew 13:15 tells us:

> For the hearts of these people are hardened,
> and their ears cannot hear,

---

16   Vengeance can be defined as: A final settlement between the Lord and those who oppose Him. It will be done with absolute justice.

17   Romans 12: 19 "Dear friends, never take revenge. Leave that to the righteous anger of God. For the Scriptures say, 'I will take revenge; I will pay them back,' says the Lord" (NLT).

and they have closed their eyes—
so their eyes cannot see,
and their ears cannot hear,
and their hearts cannot understand,
and they cannot turn to me
and let Me heal them. (NLT)

If you have hurt people like this, please tell our Lord that you now understand that you have done wrong. Ask God to forgive you and help you turn from your ways. Then decide that you won't abuse or harm another person again. He wants to help you. In His power, you can turn and be healed.

> ***Any redemption that does not take into account
> that evil occurred is no redemption at all.***"[119]

**Reflections:**

1. Do you agree with this statement: "To those who don't repent, there is judgment, even while they're here on earth"? _____
   _____

   Why, or why not? (In view of eternity, this is an important question to consider.) _____
   _____
   _____

2. Have you seen judgment come to other people's lives? _____
   _____

   Could this happen to you, at this stage of your life? _____ Why or why not? _____
   _____
   _____
   _____
   _____
   _____

4. Have you ever stopped to think what will happen to you after you die? Please take time to consider before you write your answer. _____
   _____
   _____
   _____
   _____
   _____
   _____

# SHAWSHANK REDEMPTION

The movie "The Shawshank Redemption" has a powerful image that can help you as you begin this journey of recovery. The main character, Andy Dufresne (falsely convicted of murdering his wife), has spent almost twenty years digging a tunnel through his cell wall into an equipment area. On the night of his escape, he busts a clay sewer pipe that eventually leads him to freedom. Red, a prisoner of over thirty years, in awe of his friend's accomplishment, narrates Andy's escape through a sewer pipe:

Andy crawled to freedom through 500 yards of ....foulness I can't even imagine, or maybe I just don't want to. Five hundred yards... that's the length of five football fields, just shy of a half a mile.

The power of the scene grips me every time I watch it. Andy crawls out of the pipe, strips off his sewage-soaked prison clothes and stands in the cleansing rain—arms outstretched, devouring the sweet taste of freedom for the first time in almost twenty years.

The same thing is true for the path of recovery. It begins with a 500-yard crawl through the raw sewage of our lives. Many, upon getting their first whiff, crawl back to the familiarity of their prison cell, unable or unwilling to face the pain of looking back on what they have done and what has been done to them. A few brave souls climb into the sewer line unsure of whether or not they can make it to the other end, but determined never to return to the prison cell of their addiction. Every inch is painful, yet they continue the journey because they believe at the end of the pipe, there is cleansing and there is freedom.

As one who has made that journey, I can tell you confidently, there is freedom, there is cleansing and there is hope. I will also tell you that as hard as the journey may be, the worst day in recovery is better than the best day in the addiction. I pray you will choose to climb into the pipe and endure whatever you must in order to experience the cleansing rain on the other side.

By Darrell Brazell
*www.newhope4si.com*
New Hope for Sexual Integrity, pg. 14.

## What Do I Do *NOW?*

God wants to heal victims of sexual abuse and those who have abused. The Lord wants His people to live a full and fruitful life and to have the complete destiny He has planned for them. This includes you.

It is hard work to feel the pain, to go through the anger, forgiveness, and everything that is required for healing and a changed life. Yet with God's help, it can be done.

Invite Him to help you wrestle through anything that keeps you from giving yourself totally and fully to Him; then start crawling through that sewer pipe. He will be there waiting for you with open arms.

## Steps to Recovery

Here are some additional thoughts and hope for recovery:

1. **Find a recovery group.** Celebrate Recovery (CelebrateRecovery.com) is a biblical and balanced program that helps overcome hurts, hang-ups, and habits. It is based on the actual words of Jesus rather than psychological theory. It was designed to help those struggling with hurts, habits and hang-ups by showing them the loving power of Jesus Christ through a recovery process. Celebrate Recovery is now in over 20,000 churches worldwide.

> *"Transform the pain or transfer the pain" (anonymous)*

2. Find a good **one-on-one counselor or chaplain** to work with. He or she can help you face your issues and the damage that has been done. Counseling also helps in doing the deep root work of finding out and healing what is driving your struggle or addiction.[120] There will be anger, pain, shame and denial to deal with. We need to place these negative feelings at the foot of the cross when we repent. Others have hurt you too, deeply, I would imagine.[121] Forgive them so that you may be free. Then receive His peace and freedom and His forgiveness from your sins. All these are promised to you because of what Jesus did at the cross. A good one-on-one counselor or chaplain will also help you by giving you someone to whom you can be accountable.

3. **Give yourself tight boundaries** around areas of sin. Set boundaries for your weakest moment, not your strongest. Boundaries can bring you

freedom. If you follow them, boundaries will keep you away from the danger. Along with the boundaries give yourself meaningful consequences that you will really dislike. It will help you remember your failures and assist you in making good choices.

When you think of things to avoid, start with MAP.

M = Masturbation
A = Adultery
P = Porn

> ***Give yourself tight boundaries around areas of sin.***

Also, anything that comes in through your eyes is especially powerful because men are wired to respond to visual stimulation. Turn off the TV and the movies. Monitor the lyrics to the songs you hear. Do they encourage purity? If not, change the station.

4. **Consider future consequences** before you act. When you find yourself deciding between two actions please consider what impact your choices will have on your future. People who are willing to sacrifice their immediate needs to secure future benefits make better choices. They are less likely to engage in negative behaviors and they increase desirable behaviors.

Scientific studies show that if people consider future consequences when making decisions, they are more likely to choose healthy behaviors, are more likely to resist unhealthy temptations and are able to persist in doing difficult or tedious activities.[122]

> ***Slow down your life to speed up your recovery.***

5. **Talk every day to someone** who is involved with your recovery process. Opening up to someone else can be very freeing and cleansing. It's been said that your sickness can't be entirely removed until your deepest secret is purged. Select a person (or two) that can give you wise, honest advice. It's hard to see all your own issues. They can help you understand your patterns of sin and help you establish a new and healthy lifestyle.

6. **Find good recovery material** and work on it every day (every single day).[123]

Here are some helpful books: *100 Days On The Road To Grace: A Devotional For The Sexually Broken* by Mike Genung; *Healing the Wounds of Sexual Addiction* by Dr. Mark Laaser; *Freedom Begins Here* (Devotional Journal) by Pat Springle; and *Sex, God and Men: A Godly Man's Road Map to Sexual Success* by Dr. Douglas Weiss.

See the Books and Resources listing on page 251 for more recommendations.

*The Lord is near to the brokenhearted, and saves the crushed in spirit.*

*Psalm 34:18*

**Tell Someone About Your Struggle. Don't Let Shame Keep You Trapped**

**www.purityproject.com**

7. Recognize the severity of the issue for what it truly is. **Give yourself at least 90 to 120 days** to *begin* this healing, repentance, and redemption process. It will take 3-5 years to be "street ready," *but it will be worth it to be free.*

> "You can't whitewash your sins and get by with it;
> you find mercy by admitting and leaving them."[124]

---

**With confession and accountability come freedom.**

---

The **result of our hard labor** is a changed person who is filled with healthy self-respect, a good attitude, and healthy boundaries. This person produces things of value for God's kingdom. Self-respect, especially, is something no one can take from you.

This process of restoration and healing is even harder if you can't depend on support from the ones you feel you need the most. Your healing does not depend on the ones who may have turned their backs on you. God is your healer, not man.

Many times we may want to quit – many times. God in His mercy encourages people to finish their healing process by speaking to them through a dream, Scripture, or the encouraging words of another person. He will give you help when you simply ask Him.[18]

"The man who walks with God always gets to his destination."[125]

Reset your life's path. Deal with your current issues and addictions so your life is right in the eyes of God and the others joining you in this process. Set new goals for your life, and then move forward into that change. You will be richly rewarded if you do.

---

### *If You Just Don't Quit, You Win*

---

### The Next Steps

After you have received some significant healing and you have support around you, you need to apologize to those you have wounded and, whenever possible, make things right. Here are some steps to help you in this challenging but necessary process.

1) **Begin praying** for the one (or ones) you want to ask to forgive you. Ask God to begin preparing their heart to receive what you have to say. Ask God to begin healing them from the deep wounds that are hurting them.

2) **If your actions have hurt or damaged someone,** openly admit it to them. (For example: "I'm sorry. I blew it. I know I've really hurt you. I was only thinking of myself.") Do not give any excuses or blame others. This step is necessary for your healing, and theirs too.

3) If you **ask God to help you**, He will give you the right words. You may write them or speak them from your heart. Let me say again that it's important that you don't make any excuses or blame those you have harmed.

---

18   It is God's Spirit that gives us the power to change. "Not that we are sufficient of ourselves to think of anything as being from ourselves, but our sufficiency is from God," (2 Corinthians 3:5, NKJV).

4) **Ask those you have harmed to please forgive you**. Forgiveness is important in everyone's healing. Humbling yourself and admitting your mistakes will shape your character in a way that will not allow you to easily forget and return to your past. Being truly sorry helps a person change his heart and life.

5) In reconciliation, both parties need to agree about the issue that separated them. When you ask your victims to forgive you, **tell them that you know they are hurting from what you did**. Recognize that your actions have had a significant, long-term impact on them. Tell them this truth, being sorry for it from your heart. Genuine sorrow from the heart can be given by God or can happen when you gain some understanding of how much your actions have harmed someone. Let this understanding go deep within you.

6) **Do something to make wrong things right.** Be creative on this. What would be of benefit to them? This might include an offer to pay for counseling, medical treatment, or getting training for job skills. Support their healing process in any way you can. Saying "I am sorry" is not enough. The wounded one needs to feel and know you are really sorry.

*"Sympathy is no substitute for action."*[126]

7) **Accept the consequences of your actions**. Sometimes people you harmed will not forgive you. They need to see evidence of genuine repentance, or a change in your heart and actions over time. Sometimes they will forgive you but not trust you enough to allow you back in their lives. You must accept their decision. Your joy will come as you pursue integrity and transformation and see your life radically changed. Their feelings of being betrayed can actually heal as they watch you make changes. Forgiveness and personal change will impact them deeply, as well as impacting you.

8) **Legal consequences.** Sometimes confession may bring legal consequences. If we are trusting God this is not a bad thing: it is a necessary thing – even though it is a difficult one. When we hide our illegal actions we are lying to ourselves and God. Psalm 66:18 says that if I cherish or hold sin in my heart, refusing to confess it, God will not hear my prayers. Prison will make you bitter or better, you choose. Only when I confessed my sins – all of them – did my healing begin. Gary Hardy[127]

**Reflections:**

1. What do you think about this statement: "The worst day in recovery is better than the best day in the addiction"? _____

   _____

   _____

   _____

   _____

   _____

2. List the first four steps to recovery that you will commit to do:

   _____

   _____

   _____

   _____

3. Write a date beside each one as a goal for when you will begin each step.

   If you have someone you trust, tell him or her (guys share with guys and girls share with girls) what your plan is and ask him to help by letting you report your progress to him. A counselor, chaplain or friend would be a good choice for this.

   ---

   *You need to feel successful in your recovery, so take it in steps – otherwise, you could get so discouraged that you walk away from the Lord.*

   ---

   Never forget, even when you have no earthly friends, Jesus is with you.

# INNER HEALING

by Darrell Brazell

As director of New Hope Recovery Ministries, I have spent the past fifteen years walking out my own recovery as well as working with individuals dealing with sexual issues. During this time I've gotten a firsthand view of many of the causes of sexual addiction. I have yet to encounter anyone who didn't have emotional damage, abuse and/or trauma, and trauma-based lies as a significant part of their story. Now, I have had many men who started the journey saying they just "liked porn" or that they chose this path because of they are just "bad to the core."  However, when we have explored their story, we have always found trauma.

Sometimes, the trauma is obvious to everyone in the room, except for them. For example, in a group session one night a man said, "I had a great childhood. Both my parents loved me, though my dad did have a little bit of an anger problem."  When I asked him what his father's anger looked like, he responded, "Well, when I was three or four he was giving me a bath and I must have been playing around too much. He got angry and held me under the water long enough that I thought I was going to drown." As he told the story, the rest of us in the room looked at him with horror and when I said, "Have you ever heard of water-boarding?" that it finally hit him that maybe his "normal" wasn't so "normal" after all.

Others may not have obvious traumas like this one, but they experienced things they were not able to handle at the time. As adults, when they look back at their memories they seem insignificant, so they dismiss them. However, the reality of emotional damage is that anytime our pain exceeds our capacity, it is damaging, no matter how trivial it may seem.

For example, we all have experiences on the playground, classroom and even at home when another child or an adult took our favorite toy, called us a name or spoke a harsh word to us. When we think about it as adults, we dismiss it as "just a kid thing." However, if as a child, we did not have the ability to understand fully what was going on, we interpreted the situation incorrectly; we believed a lie and it became a trauma in our life regardless of the real size of the event.

Our brain takes experiences of trauma (both big and small) and sweeps them under a rug. However, under that rug, they fester and grow. Our brain remembers we couldn't handle the pain at the time so it works hard to keep us from examining or even noticing the weird bump under the rug. However, we keep tripping over it because anytime anything remotely connected to the original pain comes up, the unresolved, unprocessed pain of the past comes flooding into our present.

Our brain continues to try to keep us from looking at the bump in the rug and simply finds something, or often some*one* in the present, to blame for the pain we feel. As long as we ignore the original trauma and stay focused on the pain in the present, we will continue going in circles and repeating this process.

Another critical factor is that the enemy of our souls, the Devil, is very good at inflicting evil upon us. He knows that pain is fertile soil for his lies to grow in. For example, in the first story, the enemy planted the lie; "I must be a horrible person for my own father to almost drown me." Most people hearing this story respond with anger at the father and compassion for the boy. However, until he told the story, until he saw our reactions, he had never even considered the possibility that the problem in that memory was not him being bad but his father being out of control.

That lie, "I am a horrible person", takes on a life of its own. Guess what you do when you believe you are a horrible person. You do horrible things and you hide. You don't let anyone see who you really are because after all, if they see me for who I believe I really am, they may want to hurt or drown me like my father almost did.

Until we face and heal from the traumas in our life, we will continue to re-experience them and allow the energy of the unhealed pain of our past to drive us to act out, live in confusion and self-medicate. In other words – our unhealed pain drives us again and again to what we believe will be pleasurable – this becomes an addiction.

A good way of recognizing that there may be old trauma at play is to notice times in your life when you "over-reacted," also known as "being triggered." For example, someone did or said something that should have, on a scale of one to ten, registered a two or three but you were triggered and felt it as an eight, nine or even ten. Where does that energy and pain come from? It comes from unhealed wounds in your past. We all have them, and if we want to be free of them and experience today on today's terms, we must begin facing our old pain.

> ***Our unhealed pain drives us again and again to what***
> ***we believe will be pleasurable – this becomes an addiction.***

Facing our pain can be a terrifying thing and the enemy will use that to his advantage. He wants to intimidate us into not looking at what is really driving our pain and our addictions because he knows if we understand the process that we will stop over-reacting and we will stop harming ourselves and others.

While resolving old pain and replacing lies with truth could be a book in and of itself, I want to take some space to offer some suggestions for ways to address old pain.

The first thing I encourage everyone to do is to simply write down your story or tell a friend. Sometimes all we have to do to resolve an old trauma is to look at and describe the original event and then our current overre-actions come into clear focus. For example, for many years, I lived with an inordinate amount of fear of my wife's anger. What you need to know to understand this is that I am not a small man. In high school, I was an all-state defensive tackle and now I would have to lose a few pounds to get back into my uniform. My wife is a petite five-foot and one-half inch beautiful lady whom you definitely would not turn to for help if a fight broke out.

Yet in our marriage, I spent many years attempting to manage her anger and living in terror of upsetting her. Then one day in a conversation with a mentor and friend, the Father revealed the true source of my fear which was a childhood encounter with my father. In the image I saw myself as a small, eight-year-old boy and my grown father was towering over me as an angry, scary man.

What I realized when I saw that image is that every time my wife started getting upset, I would be triggered into seeing myself as a small eight year old boy and seeing my wife, not as the pretty petite gift she is, but instead, towering over me like my father when I was eight. Literally, as soon as I made that connection, the gears fell in place and I saw things differently. I began seeing my wife's anger for what it was and not as the threat to my very existence that it felt like to me in my triggered place. I realized, I was "big" and able to stand in the midst of my wife's anger and didn't need to manage it or cower from it like I had my father's anger. Simply making that connection resolved the trigger.

However, many old traumas need more than "understanding," they need "healing." There have been other memories in my life that didn't resolve simply by writing or talking them out. At times I could see the connection to old pain, but seeing the connection didn't resolve it.

Those memories, those traumas need Jesus. This is where we need what is often referred to as "inner healing." There are a number of different ways people go about experiencing Jesus in their pain and different groups have given those ways different names, for example: Healing Prayer, Theophostic Prayer, SOZO, Immanuel Prayer, etc. We don't have the space to explore their individual differences. However, the common thread and healing power in each of them is going to Jesus with these traumas and experiencing more of Jesus' presence in our lives. (The chapter from section one, *You Saw Who at the Strip Club?* Is an example of this process.)

One of the most universal lies the enemy whispers to us is "You are on your own and all alone. No one understands. No one cares and even God is not here for you." However, one of Jesus' names is "Immanuel" which means "God with us" and His last words and last promise in the Gospel of Matthew were "I will be with you always" (Matthew 28:20).

I believe the deepest healing occurs when we ask Jesus to open the eyes of our hearts to perceive his presence in any and all places in our lives. This means instead of asking "why" a bad thing happened in my life, I instead begin by asking, "Jesus, where are You in this memory?" I have found that when I get stuck in the "why," I simply get more and more upset. However, when I seek Jesus, I often get much more than I could have ever imagined.

When I find Jesus in a painful memory I then ask Him to show me if there are any lies the enemy planted during the actual trauma. When He speaks His truth, the lies lose their power over me. (I will walk you through this process step by step, later in the chapter.)

I have experienced this countless times in my own life and in sessions with other men. Jesus loves revealing Himself to us in times we didn't think He was there, and He loves replacing the enemy's lies with His truth.

However, I don't want to mislead you. It is often a difficult journey with many twists and turns along the way, but please don't ever give up. Keep pursuing. Keep asking Jesus to reveal Himself. Keep asking Him what is the correct way. Ask Him to reveal to you anything that is blocking you from perceiving His presence. Then when He reveals what is in the way, ask Him if there is anything He wants you to do to remove it. Sometimes He will simply encourage you to ask Him to remove the obstacle. Sometimes He will ask you to renounce a vow or an agreement you have made with the enemy's work in your life. Do anything and everything He asks you to do.

For example, a very common vow many of us have made in times of pain, is "I won't ever allow anyone to get close enough to hurt me that deeply again." Guess what the enemy does with a vow like that? Not only does he use it to keep us isolated from others, he even uses it to prevent intimacy with Jesus. He uses that vow of protection to build walls that push away those people who have or might hurt us, but those walls keep Jesus away too. Sometimes, Jesus reveals vows like this one because we must renounce the vows we have made before we can feel Him drawing us close to Him. You can say something like this: "Jesus I repent and renounce the vow I made to (never get close enough to anyone to get hurt again.) I come out of agreement with that vow and ask that You would make it null and void. Help me to (know whom I should trust and whom I shouldn't in the future.)"

I do not believe Jesus will tear down walls we have built without our permission. However, once we recognize our vows, renounce them and ask Him to remove the wall, He is more than happy to crush it to dust and reveal Himself.

So with this in mind, I would like to share a basic model you can use to ask the Father to walk you into truth and into healing. You can do this on your own or with a prayer partner who helps you stay focused. If you do it on your own, I highly recommend using a journal to write down everything that comes to your mind at every step. This helps get out of the loops we often get stuck in when we try to work things out in our heads.

**Step 1: Declare Jesus' Authority.** Begin your time in prayer by declaring Jesus' authority over your time and place. Pray for Jesus to protect you during this time and declare that the enemy has no authority here. Pray that the Father would drive out the enemy and all his demons. Pray and understand that the enemy may still speak or do other things trying to interfere. If the enemy does this it is because the Father has allowed him to speak or act because the Father has a plan for using the enemy's actions and/or words against him. Ask the Father to help you see this if it happens and you will recognize the enemy's words or movements.

**Step 2: Appreciation.** Next, pray a simple prayer, "Father, please remind me of something I can appreciate. Remind me of a time I felt connected to you or of a gift You have given me." If you are not a believer in Jesus, then just recall a moment of special joy – a beautiful sunset, etc. Then start talking with the Father about whatever comes to your mind. Don't worry about whether you are "making it up." Just talk with Him about any time of closeness that comes to your mind or any gift He has given you, or your joyful moment. As you are talking about it with Him, pay attention to how your body feels. Do you sense your muscles relaxing, your breathing getting deeper, etc.? Next, give the memory a name and write that name in large letters on the top of your journaling page. For example, one of my recent Appreciations was "Thank You Card." Naming the appreciation gives our mind a concrete sense of ownership and gives you a peg on the wall to hold onto when the feelings of appreciation begin to fade. It will also provide a safe place where you can return to if you get stuck in a painful memory.

**Step 3: Ask Jesus To Give You A Sense Of His Presence Where You Are.** Ask Jesus to open the eyes of your heart so you can sense His presence with you right now. After you ask, let your heart look for Him. Some people get an image of Him in the room. Others just get a sense of His presence or just a peace that "knows He is here." Remember, Jesus said, "I am with you always, even to the end of the age[128]." The way you will know it is Him, is His presence always brings a sense of peace. If you don't get a sense of His presence, go back to step two and look for another appreciation. Going back and forth between seeking Him being with you in the present and your appreciation place will most likely help you to begin to sense His presence. If you do not, then simply ask Jesus to show you what is in the way and ask Him what you need to do, or what you need to ask Him to do, to remove what is in the way.

**Step 4: Ask Jesus Where He Wants You to Go Today.** Ask Jesus if there is a time in your life where you are ready to perceive His presence. Then begin talking with Him, and/or writing to Him anything that comes to your mind. If a memory comes up, just allow yourself to explore it. Then, while in the memory, ask Jesus to show you where He was then or where He is now. If you sense His presence then you can ask Him if there is anything He wants to show you or tell you about yourself, about Him or about anything. Write down everything you hear, see or sense.

If you don't sense His presence, that's OK. You can try several things: 1) ask Him to show you what is in the way and 2) ask Him what you need to do, or 3) ask what you need to ask Him to do for you to remove the ob-stacle. 4) when the obstacle is out of the way, ask Him again to show you

His presence. When you make a strong connection with Jesus, ask Him anything stirring in your heart. Here are a few examples:

- Ask Him if there are any lies the enemy has planted in your heart that He wants to remove today.

- Ask Him if you have made any vows that He wants to show you so you can renounce them (see instructions above) and ask Him to remove them from your life.

- Ask Him what He thinks about you and about who you are to Him.

His answers and the things He shows you will touch your heart in deep places. Be sure to write them down as they sometimes fade quickly. Continue with the process as long as Jesus directs you. Many times individuals think Jesus has already given them a great gift and want to stop. But I always encourage them to ask, "Jesus, is this what you wanted me to see today or do you have something more?"  Never quit until you sense Him saying, "This is enough for today."  He has often rewarded us with extremely rich gifts when we have had the boldness to be "greedy" and ask if there is anything more.

If you get stuck in a painful place, don't stay there and think it is up to you to pound your way out of it. Instead go back to your appreciation and reestablish your initial connection. Find Him in the room with you once again and then ask Him about the painful place. Often going back and forth will get you unstuck. However, if you are not able to get through a memory, do not quit in a stuck place. End your time by going back to your appreciation memory and thank Him for what He has shown you there.

**Step 5: Offer Him Thanks.** Once Jesus says it is time to be done, just spend a few minutes thanking Him for what He has shown you.

**Step 6:  Declare Jesus' Authority**. Boldly repeat or declare anything Jesus has told or shown you to be His. Declare it in Jesus' Name and that the enemy has no authority over it ever again. (I declare that I am accepted by Jesus and that I can trust Him to guide and protect me because He purchased that right for me when He died in my place. I come out of agreement with the lie that I am totally responsible for my protection and that I need to put up a wall between me and people wherever I go.)

Ask the Father to remind you of this new truth anytime the enemy attempts to lie about, distort or take away any territory the Father has claimed through this time of prayer and reflection. Declare it all His, in Jesus Name.

**Reflections:**

1. Are there some situations that you've thought were "no big deal" that, looking back now, seem like a bigger deal? Write one down. _____

   _____

   _____

   _____

   _____

   _____

2. What was going on with the person who wounded you that you couldn't understand as a child? _____

   _____

   _____

   _____

   _____

3. What was the lie you believed about yourself? _____

   _____

   _____

   _____

   _____

   _____

4. Get a notebook and begin the steps listed above to bring healing to this memory.

# A Man's Ultimate Destiny:
# A View from Heaven

# A MAN'S ULTIMATE DESTINY
# A VIEW FROM HEAVEN

### How Can I Be Forgiven, Anyway?

Jesus came to earth to find and to save those who do not know Him. He wants to give everyone eternal life – including YOU! But God is a just Judge, and all sinful activity has its price and that price must somehow be paid.

According to the Bible, there is only one way this price can be paid:  God will accept Jesus' payment for your sins if you repent and turn away from your harmful actions, ask Him to forgive you and believe in Jesus' death on the cross for you. Apart from Christ's suffering and death on the cross, your sinful deeds are not canceled and you are condemned forever to suffer for your unforgiven sins.

Please understand that these are the only two options. Either your unlawful actions against God's law will be paid for by trusting in Jesus' sacrifice when He took your place of punishment at the cross, or you will pay for them yourself. There are no other options.

### The Great White Throne Judgment

The Bible says that when we die, we must all appear before God to have our lives evaluated. One reason I wrote this book was to give you the information you need to make sure that on Judgment Day, He will welcome you as a son or daughter into His kingdom.

The Bible says that when we die, we must all appear before God to have our lives evaluated. I am very concerned for your soul on Judgment Day as you stand before the Throne of God. I don't like to see people suffering; I'd like to know you are headed for glory.

Each person without Christ will receive a final eternal judgment. The Judge of this heavenly courtroom is fair, and He will pass sentences based only on truth. There will not be a debate about innocence or guilt. There will be no defender and no jury. There will only be convincing evidence. Every sin from earth is recorded in His books. These will be judged by His holy rules. The guilty will be punished *forever* in Hell, without possibility of parole or escape. It is the eternal punishment of the unsaved. I do not want that to happen to you.

But through Christ we can escape the penalty of our deeds *and receive eternal life*. He died for *all* our evil deeds, from the little ones to the worst secret ones. He sets us free from our heavy burden of guilt for past deeds and gives us a full life here on earth and then eternal life in Heaven.

Each one needs to decide whether to turn from his sinful ways and receive God's gift of forgiveness, or whether he will stand before the Judge ready to pay for his own sin. There is simply no other way. Those who reject Christ's death as payment for their harmful activities will experience His judgment[129] and will "dwell with devouring flames"[130] for all eternity.

Dear reader, no matter what you have done, and no matter how many times you have done it, Christ's death on the cross *is enough for you now* because Jesus' death on the cross was stronger than your misdeeds, sins and mistakes. Reach out to the risen Jesus, confess to Him what you have done, and receive His forgiveness. He will make you feel clean inside and help you to make changes that are too hard for you to make by yourself. He will give you His purity. Jesus will be your guide, comforter, and helper. Just ask Him.

*"God is willing to make the best of us,*
*but we have to be willing to give*
*Him the worst of us."[131]*

Reach out to Him now by praying this prayer:

### Salvation Prayer
Jesus, I believe You are the Son of God.
I confess that I have broken Your holy laws of love.
I need Your forgiveness.
I believe that You shed Your blood and died
on the cross to pay for my sins.
I believe that You rose from the dead
and are hearing this prayer. I ask you to forgive me and wash
away my sinful acts with Your blood.
I choose to completely reject my sinful ways and

leave these works of darkness behind.
I make a choice to follow Your ways the rest of my life.
Come into my life, fill me with Your Spirit and Your love,
and be my Lord.
In Your wonderful Name,
Amen

If you prayed that prayer, continue daily to make an *unconditional and total commitment* to Jesus Christ. Determine to follow Him and His ways as one of His very own. This commitment will keep your heart from wandering in the future and will keep you on the pathway of faith, life, and love.

If you turned from your old ways and received Christ in your life with an honest heart, you are a Christian, a follower of Christ. You are born again by His Spirit and have begun a genuine friendship with Jesus, your Savior.

You may feel different after you pray, or you may feel nothing at all. It doesn't matter. If you truly gave up your sins and surrendered your whole life to Christ, then your name is written in the Book of Life. You are my brother in Christ! We are joined together in the family of God.

> **"Anyone who belongs to Christ has become a new person.
> The old life is gone; a new life has begun!"**[132]

Begin by walking away from sin and into your new life of faith as an obedient Christian. Using The Navigator's wheel[133] you can see what daily disciplines would draw you into a closer walk with God.

We also encourage you to find a good Pastor or Chaplain for your new journey of faith in Jesus Christ.

Jesus truly gives amazing grace:

### *Amazing Grace*

John Newton (1725-1807)

Amazing grace, how sweet the sound,
That saved a wretch like me.

I once was lost but now am found,
Was blind, but now I see.

T'was grace that taught my heart to fear
And grace, my fears relieved.
How precious did that grace appear
The hour I first believed.

Through many dangers, toils and snares
I have already come;
'T'was grace that brought me safe thus far
And grace will lead me home.

The Lord has promised good to me.
His word my hope secures.
He will my shield and portion be,
As long as life endures.

Yea, when this flesh and heart shall fail,
And mortal life shall cease,
I shall possess within the veil,
A life of joy and peace.

When we've been there ten thousand years
Bright shining as the sun.
We've no less days to sing God's praise
Than when we'd first begun.

Amazing grace, how sweet the sound,
That saved a wretch like me. I once was lost but now am found,
Was blind, but now I see.

## Reflections:

1. List the only way that the price of sin can be paid: _____

_____

_____

Accepting Christ's death for our past sins frees us from the penalty of our sins, making us sons and daughters of God. We are adopted into His family.

2. Do you believe that Jesus Christ forgave your sins? _____

Take some time and mention to God each sin by name, seeking His forgiveness and cleansing of each one. You will never regret taking the time to do this.

3. If you have not done so yet, pray now, asking Jesus to forgive your sins and surrender control of your life over to Him. Ask Him to be your Lord and Savior.

If you have made this life-changing decision to follow Christ, congratulations! Begin your walk with God. . .

# WORDS OF HOPE FOR YOU:
# POSITIVE CONFESSIONS

After turning control of your life over to Jesus, you might feel totally different or you might feel exactly the same. Your feelings don't matter. What matters is the truth. If you've given your life over to God, He says that you are a NEW person. He has a lot to say about who you are now and how your past has been forgiven and left behind.

An area that often causes new believers to stumble is our thought life. We all have negative thoughts that have become habits. Many of the things you have believed about yourself are now no longer true. It's VERY IMPORTANT that you learn who God says you are. You must break free from hearing critical voices from your past, or your own negative self-talk, and especially from the lies that the devil and his demons whisper in your ear to trip you up.

The Bible says that we must take every thought captive (2 Corinthians 10:5). Many times the exact opposite has happened -- our thoughts have held us as prisoners. It's time for that to change. When an old thought comes to accuse you, you need to RECOGNIZE it as a lie. RENOUNCE it and REPLACE it with the new truth of who you are now -- not who you *feel* like you are, but who Jesus says you are.

For example: "I take the thought captive that I will never be free from pornography. This is a lie and I renounce and reject it in Jesus' name. I replace this lie with the truth that I am free from sin, that I am strong in the

Lord and that I am a victor. The Lord will deliver me from all my temptations."

This can be a very slow and frustrating process. Realize that you will be tearing down thought patterns that have been in place for a long time. But if you don't learn to think new thoughts, you'll find it very hard to learn new behaviors. Proper actions are the result of proper thoughts. Healthy actions follow healthy thoughts; bad behavior follows bad thoughts. I can't tell you how important this is. **To act in new ways, you must think new thoughts. You need to form new positive thought patterns to replace the old lies that have kept you trapped.**

Please read this entire section and then concentrate on a different statement each day. At the end of a month you will see change beginning in your life.

**In Christ, I am God's child.** I am born again, not of flesh and blood (from my parents), but of God's incorruptible seed through the Word of God which abides forever (I Peter 1:23; John 1:12). I am a child of God. I am His!

**In Christ, I am forgiven.** My sins are forgiven because Jesus shed His blood for me on the cross (Ephesians 1:7; Hebrews 9:14; Colossians 1:14; 1 John 2:12; 1 John 1:9).

**In Christ, I am a new creation.** Therefore, if anyone is in Christ, the new creation has come: The old has gone. . . (2 Corinthians 5:17).

**In Christ, I am the righteousness of God.** He gives me His righteousness as a gift. "God made Him who had no sin to be sin for us, so that in Him we might become the righteousness of God. (Amazing!) (2 Corinthians 5:21).

**In Christ, I am His temple.** The Holy Spirit lives inside me (I Corinthians 6:19).

**In Christ, I am rescued from the power of darkness** (Colossians 1:13).

**In Christ, I am redeemed** from the curse of the law, of trying to get close to God by being "good enough" or performing well. "Christ redeemed us from the curse of the law by becoming a curse for us . . ." (Galatians 3:13).

**In Christ, I am blessed.** By faith, I share in the same blessings that God promised to Abraham (Galatians 3:9).

**In Christ, I am a saint,** set apart for the Lord and His kingdom (Romans 1:7; I Corinthians 1:2).

**In Christ, I am holy and blameless** before Him in love, and chosen by Him before the creation of the world (Ephesians 1:4).

**In Christ, I am firmly established to the end.** I will be counted free from all sin and guilt on that day when He returns (His Second Coming), (I Corinthians 1:8).

**In Christ, I am brought closer to God** through the blood of Christ (Ephesians 2:13).

**In Christ, I am victorious.** I am an overcomer in Christ Jesus (Revelation 21:7).

**In Christ, I am set free.** When I know the truth, the truth will set me free (John 8:31-33).

**In Christ, I am strong in the Lord.** My strength comes from the Lord's mighty power within me. It is not my own (Ephesians 6:10).

**In Christ, I am dead to sin.** He personally carried the load or burden of my sins in his own body when he died on the cross, so that I can be finished with sin and live to and for God, in freedom (Romans 6:2, 11; I Peter 2:24).

**In Christ, I am a co-heir with Christ.** "Now if we are children, then we are heirs—heirs of God and co-heirs with Christ, if indeed we share in his sufferings in order that we may also share in his glory" (Romans 8:17).

**In Christ, I am sealed with the Holy Spirit of Promise.** I am marked by the Holy Spirit as belonging to Christ (Ephesians 1:13).

**In Christ, I am accepted.** Christ has welcomed and accepted me as a member of His family (Romans 15:7).

**In Christ, I am complete in Him.** I have everything I need when I have Him (Colossians 2:10).

**In Christ, I am crucified.** "I have been crucified with Christ and I no longer live, but Christ lives in me. The life I now live in the body, I live by faith in the Son of God, who loved me and gave himself for me" (Galatians 2:20).

**In Christ, I am alive.** I was spiritually dead and doomed to Hell because of my sins. Christ has given me new life (Ephesians 2:5).

**In Christ, I am free from condemnation.** Christ has magnificently freed me from the tyranny of living under guilt and condemnation (Romans 8:1).

**In Christ, I am reconciled to God.** God brought me to Himself through what Christ Jesus did on the cross for me (2 Corinthians 5:18).

**In Christ, I am qualified to share in His inheritance.** Christ has made me fit to share all the wonderful things that belong to those who live in the Kingdom of Light (Colossians 1:12).

**In Christ, I am firmly rooted.** I am growing in the Lord and becoming strong and vigorous in the truth by faith (Colossians 2:7).

**In Christ, I am a fellow citizen.** I am a member of God's very own family, a citizen of God's country, and a member of His household (Ephesians 2:19).

**In Christ, I am born of God** and the evil one does not harm me (I John 5:18).

**In Christ, I am His faithful follower.** I am His called, chosen and faithful follower (Revelation 17:14).

**In Christ, I am overtaken with blessings.** He has blessed me with every blessing in heaven because I belong to Him and obey His voice (Deuteronomy 28:2).

**In Christ, I am His disciple.** My love for others will prove to the world that I am His disciple (John 13:34-35).

**In Christ, I am the light of the world.** I am like a city on a hill, glowing in the night so everyone can see (Matthew 5:14).

**In Christ, I am the salt of the earth** I'm like salt-seasoning that brings out the God-flavors of this earth (Matthew 5:13, The Message).

**In Christ, I am a partaker of His divine nature.** Through these he has given us his very great and precious promises, so that through them you may participate in the divine nature, having escaped the corruption in the world caused by evil desires (2 Peter 1:4).

**In Christ, I am called of God.** He has saved us and called us to a holy life— not because of anything we have done but because of his own purpose and grace (2 Timothy 1:9).

**In Christ, I am His ambassador.** God is using me to encourage others to receive the love, forgiveness and life He offers (2 Corinthians 5:20).

**In Christ, I am God's workmanship** created in Christ Jesus for good works, which God prepared in advance for us to do. God has a plan for my life (Ephesians 2:10).

**In Christ, I am the apple of my Father's eye.** "In a desert land He found him, in a barren and howling wasteland. He shielded him and cared for him; He guarded him as the apple of His eye." God protects me in the howling wasteland because I am the apple of His eye (Deuteronomy 32:10; Psalms 17:8).

**In Christ, I am a member of the body of Christ.** I am a separate and necessary part of Jesus' family (I Corinthians 12:27).

*Quite possibly you lacked a father who tenderly met your needs. Those wounds can be healed when you realize that God is the ultimate Father and He loves you.*

**In Christ, I have been adopted as a child of God.** His unchanging plan was always to send Jesus Christ to die for me so He could adopt me into His own family. It was His good pleasure to do so (Ephesians 1:5).

**In Christ, I have received the Spirit of adoption** by whom we cry out, "Abba, Father." I can freely call Him "My Father" (Romans 8:15).

**My Father knows exactly what I need.** He knows what I need even before I ask Him (Matthew 6:8).

As a father has compassion on his children, so **the Lord has compassion on those who fear Him** (fear here means holy reverence and awe). He is a Father to me, tender and sympathetic (Psalms 103:13).

I want to remind you again, you are all these things whether you *feel* like it or not. This is the truth that God has spoken about you if you are in Christ. It is in the Bible and He cannot lie!

> God is not human, that he should lie,
> not a human being, that he should change his mind.
> Does he speak and then not act?
> Does he promise and not fulfill?

> (Numbers 23:19)

# Appendix

# WHAT DOES IT MEAN TO "GET SAVED"?

The biblical word "salvation" concerns an eternal, spiritual deliverance. When Paul told the Philippian jailer what he must do to be saved, he was referring to the jailer's eternal destiny (Acts 16:30-31). Jesus associated being saved with entering the kingdom of God (Matthew 19:24-25).

What are we saved *from*? In the Christian doctrine of salvation, we are saved from "wrath[19]," from God's punishment on sin (Romans 5:9; 1 Thessalonians 1:10; 5:9). Our sin has separated us from God, and the consequence or "wages of sin" is death (Romans 6:23). Biblical salvation refers to being delivered from the consequence of sin.

Who does the saving? Only God, through Jesus Christ, can remove sin and deliver us from sin's penalty (2 Timothy 1:9).

How does God save? In the Christian doctrine of salvation, God rescues us through Christ (John 3:17). Specifically, it was Jesus' death on the cross and His resurrection that achieved our salvation (Romans 5:10). Scripture is clear that salvation is the gracious, undeserved gift of God (Ephesians 2:5, 8) and is only available through faith in Jesus Christ (Acts 4:12).

How do we receive salvation? We are saved by *faith*. First, we must *hear* the gospel—the good news of Jesus' death and resurrection (Ephesians 1:13). Then, we must *believe* - fully trust - the Lord Jesus Christ (Romans 1:16). This involves repentance[20] -- a changing of mind about sin, and with God's grace completely turning away from all known sin and then turning *to* Christ (Acts 3:19), calling on the name of the Lord Jesus (Romans 10:9-10, 13).

A definition of the Christian doctrine of salvation would be "The deliverance, by the grace of God, from eternal punishment for sin which is granted to those who accept by faith God's conditions of repentance and faith in

---

19   Wrath is defined as: retributory punishment for an offense or a crime:  divine chastisement. Merriam-Webster Dictionary
20   Repentance is changing your mind about sin and with God's grace completely turning to Christ and away from sin - all known sin.

the Lord Jesus." Salvation is available in Jesus alone (John 14:6; Acts 4:12) and is dependent on God alone for provision, assurance, and security. [134]

Please see A Man's Ultimate Destiny: A View from Heaven for more information on how to receive salvation, on page 197.

# BREAKING UP IS HARD TO DO

Think of a time that you ended a relationship. Did you totally end it — walking away and not looking back — or did you do it halfway — out one week and back the next? Completely or halfway? It's always best when ending a relationship to walk away and never look back — it's a clean break. The other way is messy and painful. You're in, you're out, you keep going back.

When we turn our lives over to Jesus ("getting saved") it's important that we make a clean break. Don't dabble with sin and don't go back. After we repent we leave our old lifestyles, and pursue our new relationship with Him.

Are you ready to make a clean break from sin, including sexual sin, and make a clean break? Are you willing to trust Jesus to take over your life and to bring you His blessings, freedom and love? If you are, then just tell Him what you're feeling and thinking and tell Him that you give your whole life to Him — every part of it. Do it now.

What happens next is amazing. He'll forgive you and forget the sins you've committed. He'll help make you into a new person. It's an amazing trade off. Here are a few verses that promise it's true:

"And he has taken our sins as far away from us as the east is from the west" (Psalm 103:12, ERV).

"I will show loving-kindness to them and forgive their sins. I will remember their sins no more" (Hebrews 8:12, NLV).

"I am the one who wipes away all your sins. I do this to please myself. I will not remember your sins" (Isaiah 43:25, ERV).

"I will forget their sins and never again remember the evil they have done" (Hebrews 10:17, ERV).

When you get saved the Holy Spirit, the very Spirit of God, comes to live inside you to help you start over and build a new life. It's not right for us to stay involved in the same sins from which we are asking Jesus to save and forgive us from. Unfortunately you'll probably still feel some of the same desires you had before you got saved. You'll probably also feel bad if you fall back into these old patterns. That feeling is called *conviction* and it's the Holy Spirit warning you, "Don't do that. It's bad for you." In addition to bringing conviction He will also give you the strength to change. He'll help you make healthy choices.

When you fall back into old patterns, don't waste time telling yourself that you're a creep and you'll never get free. Run to Jesus and ask for His forgiveness and help in order to make a clean break with your past. You'll enjoy your new life of obedience and your new relationship with the Lord. He's waiting for you now!

### Developing a Relationship with Your Lord

How can you develop a relationship with this marvelous Savior and Lord? Here are four steps to help you begin:

1. Tell another believer about the decision you just made.[21] This is import-ant. You don't need to be a preacher to do this. Simply tell a friend or another follower of Jesus what happened.

2. Stay close to Jesus, the source of your faith. The way to do this is by talking with God, just like you'd talk to anyone else. It's called prayer. Start by thanking Him for saving you from the punishment we all deserve and then let Him know the requests of your heart. He is waiting!

3. Read the Bible every day. Scripture is often called "the bread of life." Just like we need to eat each day, we need to read daily to grow in knowledge and understanding of Jesus and His ways. Bible studies are very helpful in this area.[22]

4. Find a support group of committed followers of Jesus and get involved. This is very important. Often large churches offer these. You should not

---

21   Romans 10:9-10: "If you declare with your mouth, 'Jesus is Lord,' and believe in your heart that God raised Him from the dead, you will be saved. For it is with your heart that you believe and are justified, and it is with your mouth that you profess your faith and are saved".

22   It is good to start your Bible reading by asking for God's presence to be with you. See Luke 24:45 "And He opened their understanding, that they might comprehend the Scriptures."

be alone on your journey. The people in your support group will help you live the life you are trying hard to achieve. They will come alongside you. You will need to be involved in multiple meetings every week[135] for a long period of time, to make a clean break in the old relationships with sin.

Group involvement or group support also increases your faith, your knowledge, and helps you grow in love. Remember how other guys in this book shared that being a part of a group of committed men was absolutely necessary for them to break free of their addictions? It will be the same with you. You will walk together and become like family. These men will become your friends and encouragers. Church is a wonderful way to grow in your faith.

5. We also need to change what we see. We can't continue watching the same TV shows and movies with sexual immorality – including unmarried sex – when the Bible tells us to set no worthless thing before our eyes (Psalm 101:3).

# THREE EXAMPLES OF A TRANSFORMED LIFE

Let these three testimonies encourage you to believe that you, too, can be totally transformed by a loving God.

### A Gang Member No More

My mother used to pray for my salvation when I was a gang member. She would have a hand towel that she would wring out every hour or so because she would weep so much while asking God to break into my life. Finally, when I turned 17, I gave my life to Jesus.

The journey from being an ex-gang-member-high-school-dropout to an intercessory missionary[136] was a long, tough walk. The most difficult portion of my walk was my relationship with my mother.

After my parents divorced, it was difficult for me to ever accept my family. At times I would remember what it was like when my parents were married. I used to be disgusted as a little kid when I would see them kiss. Now I have a silver bracelet that says "Mom and Dad." That is the last present I will ever receive from both of them ever again.

Growing up, I always searched for a male role model I could imitate so I could learn how to become a man. I was mentored by gang leaders, drug lords and pimps, then by highly educated pastors, and now by radical, inner-city intercessory missionaries. However, the greatest lesson I have learned about becoming a man was the importance of honoring and praying for women, especially my mother.

My mother's prayers brought me to a place where I now believe that prayer is my most powerful weapon. I stand confident in my profession as an inner-city intercessory missionary because I know that when I was a gang member, no man could save me, no matter how great their testimony, how powerfully they spoke or how many signs and wonders may have passed through their hands. No man could have ever stopped me from my path to Hell except for Jesus through my mother's prayers.

I had only one mission, as an active gang member, and that was to go to Hell or be incarcerated for life by 21. My plan was to murder so many people that my fate with Satan would have been sealed forever. My mentor's name was "Demonio," or "Devil" in Spanish. One of the first lessons he taught me was deception; friends are easier to kill than enemies. Because my friends were leaders of my rival gangs, Demonio told me to target them first. He told me to never look for fights because if I was truly gang-bangin' (killin' other gangstas), then I would be on a hit list anyway. He prepared me as a teenager to be dead by 21 or locked in prison for life.

He became my father, because my real father was never there. I chose to give my life to my gang because of my love and loyalty to my street father, Demonio. I aimed to finish what he began as a full-time criminal. I left everything to murder and die for my gang; but my mother's prayers were more powerful than the heart of a demon-driven gang member.

I now spend my life mentoring men and women into lifestyles filled with power through intimacy with God by prayer and fasting. First Peter 3:7[23] says that men's prayers are hindered when they don't honor women. In order for men to live lives filled with power, our lives must be filled with prayer and fasting first.

I am now convinced that what marks my young spiritual manhood is the value I have for honoring and praying for my mother. I plan to spend the rest of my life training other young men to have a strong belief in justice for women.

I believe that without women's justice there cannot be true justice. I cannot fight for justice and dishonor women. For men to fight for women's justice, they must pray for women's justice. If men do not pray, then justice is not released.

Women's injustice can only be dealt with if it is dealt with in the spiritual realm first.

This nation is collapsing for many reasons, and one of the ways we will see this nation rise from the pits of its sin is by seeing young men honor and pray for the women, especially their mothers.

Anonymous, Intercessory Missionary
Hope City – International House of Prayer, Kansas City[137]
Used with permission

---

23   "Husbands, in the same way be considerate as you live with your wives, and treat them with respect as the weaker partner and as heirs with you of the gracious gift of life, so that nothing will hinder your prayers.".

## Rodney's Story

My name is Rodney Thompson. In May of 2005, I found myself at the end of a 24-year cocaine, crystal meth, and alcohol addiction. I was also addicted to the lifestyle that goes along with these things -- pornography and sex -- using women for my own personal selfish needs. I was totally broken and had lost everything: family, businesses, and even the ability to take care of myself. I was homeless.

One night as I was in a crack house, a pastor, led by the Holy Spirit, came to the house and called me outside. He talked to me about Jesus Christ which made me very uncomfortable.

Two weeks later, still in a crack house, I had a moment like the Prodigal Son in the Bible. This young man had lived foolishly, spending his money on parties and women. He lost everything and ended up with a job feeding pigs. He was really depressed but he came to his senses and realized he could return to his father as a hired servant and live in better conditions than he was currently experiencing (Luke 15:11-32).

I had the same type of moment when I came to my senses while I was figuratively eating pig slop. In this moment, I had an encounter with Jesus. He came and spoke to me. He revealed Himself to me. I was struck with how real He was and at that very moment I accepted Him on His terms. You see, for my whole life I had been turning God into my image, and the truth was God was not going to change who He was to suit my sin.

I repented. I surrendered my life and was filled with the Holy Spirit. Keep in mind that I had never read the Bible before so I had no idea what was happening to me. Next Jesus led me to a place where people taught me the right way to live.

From that day until today, my eyes have not looked at pornography. I stayed sexually pure and when I met my wife, we stayed pure until marriage. (We now have two beautiful young girls). I received a gift from the Lord that gave me the strength I needed to live my life for Jesus, to avoid sin and to tell other people about Him. When we become children of God we are given His righteousness as a free gift which keeps us from boasting about our own abilities. It is a witness of His glory.

In the Bible, choosing and following Jesus is called the "narrow way."[138] It has not been easy at times, but I believe that I am now making choices that have eternal consequences; they will affect the way I live for all eternity. If you would like to meet this Jesus, call out to Him and He will answer you. God bless.

Only God can turn:

> A mess into a message, a test into a testimony,
> a trial into a triumph, a victim into a victor.[139]

### Wearing the Overcomer's Crown

Young men growing up in this generation have it truly hard. I learned very quickly what it meant to be a teenager growing up in this age. I can write this article today because of Jesus in my life. The things I have experienced have shown me how much God truly loves me.

At an early age my family felt we'd be safer living in Orange County, so we moved out of Los Angeles. So it was "life in the suburbs." Everything was great until my father left. I was too young at the time to understand the importance of having a male role model. My older brother had to take on the role of my father. He was abusive because my father had been an abusive alcoholic. Under these conditions, I grew up to be very shy and timid.

Since giving up everything in L.A., my family was poor. When I started elementary school, I was ridiculed by my peers. They called me offensive names and referred to my brother as a prostitute. I told myself I would never be abused again, so my personality changed. I grew up to be passive/aggressive. My timidity turned into mischief and my shyness to anger. In junior high I became involved with a Korean church. It was hard for me to make friends, but there was a certain group, called "the problem kids," which did accept me. These were fellow teenagers from my church who were misjudged by a majority of the elders. We started with small mischiefs here and there, like blowing off fireworks in Bible study and starting a fight club in the basement, and other junior high pranks.

During my pre-teen years I was not fond of Asians (other than my church friends), so I decided to associate with Latinos. My friends and I were introduced to gangbanging. Gangbangers are West Coast gangsters. It meant being a part of a low-class crime syndicate, dealing with armed robbery, carjacking, extortion, drug dealing, and active warfare with other enemies. My friends and I had grown close, like family, and we all joined a gang all together.

For a while I became a "Southsider," which is a group of Latinos who were part of a larger mafia in prison. During initiation I was tested by the leaders of the gang in the areas of trust, loyalty, and courage. I needed this when the odds seemed to be against me. I was beaten or "jumped in," meaning I had to prove my loyalty by committing theft or violence. All my anger and hatred were subdued as a gangbanger. I was happy that I belonged to a family who looked out for me. However, I had an appetite for destruction, being constantly in conflict with other rival gangs. Our primary rivals were the infamous "18th Street." I was always on alert and in imminent danger. Violence, sex, graffiti, and securing drugs would be my life for a season. I was committed to my gang and this lifestyle for the long haul.

The turning point occurred at the height of my gangbanging career, when a group of men disrespected my girlfriend. Unable to control my temper, I decided to hunt down the offenders. Our gang had two cars, and in our car were the driver, armed with a switchblade, a youngster with a tire iron, and me, clutching a wooden baseball bat. My friends and I were under the influence of marijuana, crack cocaine, and alcohol when we found them.

The other gang members also had two cars. Our second car carried the firearms, an M1 rifle and a tactical pump shotgun. As their first car sped away, our second car took off after them. The car closest to us took off in the opposite direction. We took off after it and crashed our car into theirs. After almost flipping over from the impact, I felt gravity pull me back in to my seat as both cars spun out. In a dazed state, I saw six gangbangers running toward our driver's side.

Fueled only by rage, I kicked open my door and exited the car swinging my bat. Meanwhile, my best friend (the driver) was stabbed in his left lung. The youngster was stabbed in the back. I experienced what felt like three pinches to my rib cage, shoulder, and back. The shock made me drop my bat. A very bad feeling hit my gut as I was tripped and jumped, assaulted by pipes, boots, and fists. I got back up as quickly as possible to defend myself, only to be tripped and jumped again. Then I heard sirens, and with one last breath I yelled at my friends to run away. I managed to escape, but I couldn't breathe. My lungs were collapsing, and I was drowning in my own blood. I staggered to the nearest house and tried to call an ambulance, but was turned away. I decided to sit up against a wall and die.

I said my "last" prayer, thanking the Lord for people I had touched in a positive way and asking forgiveness for those I'd wronged. Lastly, I begged for salvation and fell asleep. I awakened to firemen searching me for wounds. As we raced to a hospital, I realized there *was* a God. I felt a warm blanket of love over me, a love I had never experienced before. As I recovered, I gave my life to Christ.

The road out of my gang was not easy. I was offered opportunities to join a Korean mafia. I was framed for attempted murder and faced 25 years to life without parole.

Even when I was incarcerated, I still encountered Jesus, He never left me. He was faithful to me and protected me. He heard my every cry and delivered me from my addictions. In prison, I had the time to read the Bible from cover to cover.

Because of my connections to the Korean mafia, I was well taken care of. Our Korean "Rep" (representative of the ethnic groups) was actually a believer, facing life in prison. He was very wise leader in navigating political decisions between races, to promote peace. I was discipled by him and became his left-hand man in all political operations.

> **"Because God has made us for Himself, our hearts are restless until they rest in Him."** [140]

Although I faced charges for a crime I did not commit, I am glad I did not let my heart get bitter and I was able to put my hope in Christ. I went back and forth from cell to court dates fighting my case. It looked really bad because the victim pointed me out in a photo lineup declaring that he was 100% sure I was the one who stabbed him. Already I began to prepare mentally, understanding that prison life would be my life for the next 25 years.

One day after I came back from court, I hopped in the shower to wash up and I prayed. I told the Lord that I would fully submit to His calling for my life, whether it be prison ministry or to live life as a missionary. I asked for protection and grace, then said my "Amen." I hopped out of my shower and began to put my dinner together, when the sheriffs pulled me out to tell me I was being released. My public defender, that day, was finally able to separate my case from the others involved; therefore I was released without conviction. I could not believe how quickly the Holy Spirit had responded. So from that day on and until now, I have been in ministry to reach out to the inner city in America.

I am so thankful for miracles of the past and for miracles yet to come. I am also thankful for the opportunity to give my testimony. If I had any advice, it would be as follows:

- Do not ever stop talking to God. Whether you are mad, happy, or sad, it doesn't matter.

- God is a Father to the fatherless, and He cares about you and hears you.

- Don't ever give up. In the midst of all the craziness of the world, Jesus loves you and you are going to make it.

Always remember, your testimony can change our generation.

Anonymous, Intercessory Missionary
Hope City -- International House of Prayer Kansas City
Used with permission

**Reflections:**

These authors talked about making choices. We all need to choose well. How can making long-term choices for recovery and righteousness (as compared to short-term choices called "lust" or "gotta have it now") become a reality in your life?_____

_____
_____
_____
_____
_____


List several good decisions you have made. _____

_____
_____
_____
_____
_____


How did you feel about yourself when you chose wisely? _____

_____
_____
_____
_____
_____
_____
_____
_____

# A COVENANT WITH MY EYES[141]

## by Bob Sorge

When you are walking in sexual purity your eyes are clear, your spirit is bright, your body is full of light, your heart is alive and responsive to God and you can feel the love flowing between you and Jesus. It's the best way to live.

### My Journey

Seven years ago in my daily Bible reading I came to this verse and I was praying, telling the Lord that I wanted to continue in sexual purity. To my surprise, the Lord interrupted my prayer and whispered, "You know you've never actually done this." I realized I had been saying yes without actually making the covenant.

> *A man in the Old Testament named Job, said "I have made a covenant with my eyes: why then should I look upon a young woman?" (Job 31:1)*

In my opinion, this covenant is the most powerful tool the Bible gives us for sexual purity. A covenant is much more serious than making a commitment. The word *covenant* is a "sledgehammer" word. It's a serious verbal or written pledge that must never be broken. When a covenant is broken, consequences can happen.

I took a week and prayed and felt that the Lord had given me an invitation and a gift of grace to help keep this covenant. I wrote the covenant, dated it, put it in my journal and gave a big financial offering to remember it by. Then I panicked, *Oh, my gosh, what did I just commit to?* But after I made the covenant, I noticed an immediate difference and it has never gone away.

I have several reasons for wanting to walk in purity but the main reason is that I want to see God. Drawing near to Him is my life's goal. It's my passion. Job made this covenant and he saw God face-to-face. Job said, "I have heard of you by the hearing of the ear, but now my eyes see you," (Job 42:5). Matthew 5:8 states, "Blessed are the pure in heart for they shall see God." I want you to see God, too.

## A Daily Fight

As you know, sexual purity doesn't come without a fight. I want you to picture your life as an ancient castle. This castle represents your thoughts and the gate represents the place that sexual temptation enters—your eyes. The enemy will always attack the gate because once he gets on the inside (your mind) then the battle is over. We have to keep him on the outside where we can fight him. Unfortunately, compromise is just one mouse click away and as long as there is a crack in the eye gate you will never walk in purity. Second Corinthians 10:5 tells us how we can keep the enemy outside the gate, "Our battle is to bring down every deceptive fantasy and every imposing defense that men erect against the true knowledge of God. We even fight to capture every thought until it acknowledges the authority of Christ," (J. B. Phillips).

## Two Steps to Victory

Fear of consequences isn't always enough to keep us fighting the battle. I've learned it takes two things to bring victory: the Love of Christ and the fear of the Lord. Let me change examples now. Let's look at your life as a car. In order to drive safely, you need a gas and a brake pedal. The gas pedal moves you forward in the right direction and a brake pedal stops you from going in the wrong direction. The gas pedal is the love of Christ and the brake is the fear of the Lord.

The first step is to abandon your heart, in love, to Jesus and it will drive you forward into an unshakable relationship with Him. When you use the gas pedal of love to press forward into obedience, Jesus understands it's an expression of your love to Him. It increases your intimacy with Jesus. As you devote yourself to prayer, and reading and meditating on the Bible, the gas pedal of love will accelerate you forward into obedience, purity and faith. Sin hinders your ability to receive God's love but obedience increases it.

To drive a car successfully you also need a brake. There is only one brake that will stop you from crashing into sin and it's not the fear of getting caught. It's the fear of the Lord. Do you tremble in the presence of the holiness, majesty, power, justice and jealousy of God? You should, because He's a God who punishes sin, judges the wicked and disciplines His children. He's greatly to be feared. If you don't tremble before the fear of the Lord, don't make this covenant.

## Scared Spitless

The whole point is to make a covenant that scares you so badly that it brings you to a full stop when you are tempted. Making a covenant with your eyes should make you tremble all over. It should scare you spitless—because you understand how serious it is to make a covenant with God. It's the fear of the vow that helps us keep it. The fear is the brake; it's the fear of God Himself. He's a consuming fire. I tremble at the thought of His judgment and it makes me cry out, "No! Get behind me, Satan!" Your flesh actually wants to look at that image but you don't because you're just too scared. It's this fear factor that gives you strong brakes. It catapults you into another level of victory.

If you don't have this fear, ask God to give it to you. It is terrifying and glorious. It's His kindness to keep you, restrain you, preserve you and direct you. Ask for more.

Because of this frightening nature, vows should be entered into slowly and carefully. Here are five reasons that making an eye covenant is so scary:

1. It involves our sexuality. For many, this is their area of greatest failure and shame.

2. Knowing our weakness, we realize we can't fulfill this on our effort alone. We must daily depend on the Holy Spirit for victory and that can be scary.

3. Because of the One with Whom we're making the covenant. We're making a solemn promise with God, the all-powerful ruler of the universe, who takes no pleasure in fools.

4. A vow provides no room for failure. There is no provision for blowing it. When you got married you didn't have a clause that allowed you to have an affair.

5. Because the Bible doesn't let us back out. Once you make it, you are in it for as long as you made the vow.

## Is There Any Good News?

By now you might be asking, "Gee, Bob, what's the good news?" There's plenty of good news.

1. Vows get God involved in a greater way in your pursuit of purity. He's saying, "If you'll go there, I'll go there with you." He gives you more and more help.

2. Vows help us by giving us strength. If you are tempted, the vow helps you stay strong.

3. A vow that you keep will take your intimacy to another level. I promise myself to Him and He promises Himself to me. It's beautiful.

4. It has the power to take you over the summit into a new level of victory in the grace of God. Most believers stay stuck, just gritting their teeth and trying harder in their own power.

## Breaking the Vow, or Bumps in the Road?

By now you might be asking, "What happens if I break my vow?" My answer is, "I don't know." If you make a marriage vow and you commit adultery you don't know what your spouse will do. She might forgive you, she might not. She might separate from you, she might divorce you, she might hire a hit man. In the Bible, when people broke vows, God punished some of them, some He begged to return to Him, and some He killed.

> *When you are walking in sexual purity your eyes are clear,*
> *your spirit is bright, your body is full of light, your heart*
> *is alive and responsive to God and you can feel the love*
> *flowing between you and Jesus.*

Before you stop reading, let me say that I see a difference between breaking your vow and hitting a bump along the way. Let me give you an example using the marriage vow. If someone had lustful feelings toward another woman and felt terrible about it and went to his wife and confessed and said, "Will you pray with me about it?" this is a bump. Saying, "I slept with another woman last night would you please pray for me?" breaks the vow.

Here's another example. Breaking your vow would be going to a porn site on the internet. Now let's say I was in the check-out line at the grocery store and noticed the magazines on my left and then I turn my head away. This actually happened to me and after I looked away the muscles in my neck that I didn't know existed caused me to take a second look. The first look was unplanned; it was OK. The second look was not allowed; it was a bump. So right there in the grocery store I prayed, "Lord forgive me I don't want it to be like this. I don't want to take the second look. Help me; cleanse me." It was a bump, you repent, He forgives you and helps you to keep moving forward.

When you're bumping your way through your eye covenant He is not like a referee just waiting to throw a penalty flag. He's overcome with love for you. He's delighted over the covenant you've made. His heart moves toward you and is celebrating your choices. He is your biggest cheerleader. He loves the ways you set your eyes on Him.

By the way, this vow is universal. It's available for men and women. Unfortunately more and more women are struggling with the issues of porn and lust. Ladies, it's just as effective for you as it is for the men.

### How Long?

Vows can be lifelong or for a specific period of time. I'd encourage you not to make a lifetime vow right away. Ask the Lord about this because it's a serious commitment. You can start by making a covenant with your eyes for a day. Test drive it and enjoy the victory and then make a covenant for three days and enjoy the victory and then make it for a month and then a year. By the end of the year I think you'll sign up for the rest of your life because you'll enjoy grace and empowerment from the Lord.

### A Sample Vow

Count the cost up front, make a covenant and obey it all the days of your life.

Here's a sample for a 24-hour vow:

> Heavenly Father for the next 24 hours I make a covenant before You with my eyes. I vow to never let my eyes settle upon a woman or man to lust. When I unexpectedly encounter a seductive image or someone I'm attracted to, I will either look away, turn it off, or walk away. I focus my eyes on Jesus only, and set my mind on things above, where Christ is, sitting at the right hand of God. Please remind me

continually of this covenant vow, and grant me the grace to keep it. Knowing the weakness of my frame and the greatness of Your power, I throw myself upon Your mercy and strength. Amen.

## Purity Tools

I want to congratulate you on taking that step and encourage you to use what I call "Purity Tools".

1. Pray the Word – When Jesus was tempted in the wilderness He quoted scriptures to the Devil (Matthew 4:4-10). Collect your own scriptures to use in times of temptation.

2. Meditate on Christ – We become like what we look at or think about. If you look at porn, you'll become more addicted. If we spend time studying scriptures about Jesus and worshipping Him, we will become more like Him.

3. Fast from food - Denying your normal appetites gives you strength to resist your sinful, sexual appetites. Also, fasting tenderizes your heart toward spiritual things.

4. Accountability - Find an accountability partner who is the same sex as you and preferably older and more mature. Don't get an accountability partner who struggles in the same area.

5. Repent – Repent immediately when you hit a bump. Use Psalm 51 as you pray.

6. Make no provision for the flesh – Don't put yourself in a position to be tempted. Get rid of questionable books, magazines, DVD's, CD's, music, cancel cable TV, etc. Don't go to bars or hang out with people who pressure you to compromise. Get filtering software for your computer. Check out the list of resources in the back of this book.

## Psalm 51

Psalm 51 was written by King David after he committed adultery and then had the woman's husband murdered in order to hide his sin. David's struggle with sexual sin and his abuse of power was not considered a "small" sin, especially for the leader of a nation.

We sometimes give in to disobedience and sin. David, in this biblical story, was not able to sleep, so he went outside on the roof of his castle (overlooking other homes like a King's castle does) watching a very beautiful woman take a bath. He watched her, didn't turn his eyes away, and lusted for her, inquired about her with his staff, and then used his power to summon her to the castle.

David later confesses his sin, and repents. Psalm 51 is David's prayer of repentance. What is God's response? If we confess our sins to Him and turn from them, He is merciful. He will restore our heart and cleanse our spirit. He washes us, and He forgives us for the bad things we have done.

Pray these words from your heart to the God who longs to forgive you and help you leave your sins behind:

God, show me your favor
in keeping with your faithful love.
Because your love is so tender and kind,
wipe out my lawless acts.
Wash away all of the evil things I've done.
Make me pure from my sin.

I know the lawless acts I've committed.
I can't forget my sin.
You are the one I've really sinned against.
I've done what is evil in your sight. . . then I will be clean.
Wash me. Then I will be whiter than snow.
Let me hear you say, "Your sins are forgiven."
That will bring me joy and gladness. . .
God, create a pure heart in me.
Give me a new spirit that is faithful to you. . .
Give me back the joy that comes from being saved by you.
Give me a spirit that obeys you. That will keep me going.

Then I will teach your ways to those who commit lawless acts.
And sinners will turn back to you. . .

If you are interested in knowing more about dissociation, here's an article that explains it in more detail . . .

# DISSOCIATIVE IDENTITY DISORDER[142]

Formerly called Multiple Personality Disorder, Dissociative Identity Disorder (DID) is a unique psychological condition in which the mind splits itself into multiple identities in order to cope with overwhelming childhood trauma. Amnesic barriers are generally erected between the identities that are formed to enable some parts of the person to be sheltered from the reality of the abuse and thus able to maintain a sense of normalcy in an otherwise intolerable situation. These shielded identities are then able to function in everyday life without being encumbered with the effects of the trauma.

Only a very immature psyche will respond to extreme trauma by creating separate identities. Therefore, DID occurs only in individuals whose trauma *began* before the age of 5 or 6. Once the psyche initiates this type of defense, however, it can continue to create more identities throughout life -- whenever it serves a beneficial purpose.

Rather than being a true mental illness, DID actually represents a marvelously creative defense mechanism employed by extremely traumatized children. When they had no way of *external* escape, they found a way to escape the intolerable events *internally*. The condition bears the negative connotation of "disorder" only because its smooth operation often breaks down later in life. Disturbing memories, emotions, and behaviors begin seeping through weakened dissociative barriers, interfering with normal daily living and alerting the unsuspecting Primary Presenter, or Host identity, that something is wrong. This is what usually motivates survivors to seek help.

Thankfully, DID is usually treatable in the hands of a knowledgeable therapist and with the proper motivation and cooperation of the survivor.

The journey to healing and wholeness is generally an extended and difficult process, however. It requires identifying and resolving the intolerable psychological conflicts which seemingly necessitated the dissociation so that the survivor can own (his or) her entire history, including the previously unbearable events. In cases of ritual abuse, varying degrees of mind-control programming and demonization are also involved and further complicate the healing process.

The phenomenon of dissociation lies on a continuum; however, that progresses to conditions which become increasingly more pathological and disruptive to normal functioning. Dissociative Identity Disorder in the most extreme form, involving the complete splitting of the soul. Since the soul encompasses the mind, will, and emotions of the person, each split-off part will have an independently functioning mind, will, and capacity for emotions.

This most extreme form of dissociation occurs when an immature child (under the age of seven) experiences a distressing event of unbearable magnitude from which (he or) she is powerless to escape physically. (He or) she also cannot use normal dissociation to disengage (his or) her mind as a whole from the reality occurring in (his or) her external environment because (his or) her brain is not programmed to handle the event on its own.

So somehow at this intolerable and inescapable moment of time, God enables this totally overwhelmed child to split off a part of (his or) her soul so that only a small, separated portion has to endure the unbearable trauma in the external environment while (he or) she, i.e. the Original Self, escapes conscious awareness of the event. With an amnesic barrier separating (him or) her from the trauma-bearing "alter-identity," the Original Self is thus able to continue life unaware of the intolerable event and seemingly unaffected by it.[143]

# DELIVERANCE FUNDAMENTALS [144]

by Lee Harms

- **Deliverance is** the process of someone being set free from the direct influence of evil spirits.

- **Demons are not** spirits of the dead sent back to earth. They are (definitely) expressions of evil as they are connected to the primary evil being himself – Satan.

They do seem to have a personality of sorts that constantly seeks to express itself by occupying a person and influencing their thoughts or deeds. They are 'driven', compulsive beings that are compelled to exercise their evil influence on humans.

- **We must have the person's permission and cooperation.**

- **Are demons for real?**
    - Ephesians 6:12 *For we do not wrestle against flesh and blood, but against principalities, against powers, against the rulers of the darkness of this age, against spiritual hosts of wickedness in the heavenly places.*

- **Can a Christian be directly influenced by a demon?** Yes.
    - 1 Cor. 12:10 . . . *to another the working of miracles, to another prophecy, to another discerning of spirits, to another different kinds of tongues, to another the interpretation of tongues.*

    - Mark 7:24-30 (children's bread)[145]

- **Characteristics of demons**
    - *They have a will:* Mtt. 12:43-45 *"I will return" "When an*

*unclean spirit goes out of a man, he goes through dry plac-
es, seeking rest, and finds none. Then he says, 'I will return
to my house from which I came.' And when he comes, he
finds it empty, swept, and put in order. Then he goes and
takes with him seven other spirits more wicked than himself, and they enter and dwell there; and the last state of
that man is worse than the first. So shall it also be with this
wicked generation."*

- o They desire a body: Mark 5:1-14 they can speak through someone[146]

- o They exhibit emotions: Mark 5:7 they caused crying and pleaded on their own behalf:

    *And he cried out with a loud voice and said, "What have I
    to do with You, Jesus, Son of the Most High God? I implore
    You by God that You do not torment me." For He said to
    him"Come out of the man, unclean spirit!" 9 Then He asked
    him, "What is your name?" And he answered, saying, "My
    name is Legion; for we are many."*

- **What demons do:** The Bible gives us many indications of activities in which evil spirits engage. Although it is not an exhaustive list, some of the more common activities are shown below.

### Activities of Demons

| ACTIVITY | REFERENCE |
|---|---|
| They entice and tempt | 1 Cor. 7:5; James 1:13-14 |
| They deceive | 1 Timothy 4:12 |
| They enslave | Romans 8:15; 2 Pet. 2:19-20; John 8:34 |
| They cause fear, timidity | 2 Tim. 1:7; 1 John 4:18 |
| They defile | Titus 1:15 |
| They teach | 1 Tim. 4:1 |
| They cause illness | Luke 13:11 |
| They do the works of Satan | Luke 11:17-19; John 8:38-41, 44 |
| They lie | John 4:44 |

We don't need to be concerned about these activities, only aware of them. The more we know of the enemy's tactics, the better equipped we are to minister to those whom he influences and resist his attempts to influence us.

- **Demons often have the right to be there** - a spiritual right - unless that door is closed. The person may not be responsible/such as in a parental entry. Some entry points are; sin, spiritual adultery, unforgiveness, trauma, curses.

## A Typical Deliverance Session:

No two sessions are alike, and we never want to get into a rut about how to minister to someone. The Holy Spirit is our guide and He can direct us to omit something we normally would do or to proceed in a certain way that we may never have done before. It is good, however, to have a general outline of how to proceed; and I offer here a general format that has proved productive for us many times.

- **Close the Open Doors**

Demons operate under the Biblical rule book, and they have a reason why they are active in somebody's life. Unless the spiritual right for the evil spirit to influence someone is removed, deliverance is normally not successful or lasting; and it is actually unwise to attempt. Let me be quick to say, however, that the demonized individual *may not* be responsible for the reason or, in some cases, they may not even be aware of the reason. In other words, don't be too quick to judge or condemn the person you are ministering to. Remember Paul's admonition to the Corinthians, *"Let all that you do be done in love"* (1 Corinthians 16:14). It is our understanding that an entry point for a demon normally takes the form of one of the following:

  o Sin - Deliberate, rebellious, repetitive sin is an open door for demonic access

  o Spiritual Adultery – When someone seeks a supernatural experience apart from those initiated by the Holy Spirit

  o Unforgiveness – Forgiving is often difficult. Forgiveness does not suggest that you must completely forget. It does not mean that you no longer feel the pain. It does not require that we cease asking for justice

- o   Trauma – Children and adults

- o   Curse – Can be generational, having been passed down through the bloodline, or specific curses hurled against someone as an act of witchcraft or black magic

- o   Command the Spirits to Leave

- o   John 4:4 "Greater is He who is in you than he who is in the world."

- o   Start where your faith level is, and let the Lord build on it from there.

- **Inner Healing**

"The process in which the Holy Spirit brings forgiveness of sin and emotional renewal to people suffering from damaged minds, wills, and emotions." John Wimber

- o   Inner healing may be needed for the person Jesus sets free to remain free. Result of inner healing should be peace.

- **Follow-up**

- o   Stay close to the Lord – And in Christian fellowship

- o   Study God's Word

- o   We need the full armor of God

- o   Spend time with God – Pray for your needs, pray in the Spirit

- o   Praise God – Praise goes before the battle

- o   Don't be afraid – You are protected by the blood of Jesus

- o   Don't abide in sin – yield to the Lord and confess your sins

- o   Don't choose to keep bad habits – Seek God about change

- o   Don't fear being tested – God allows Satan to test us not so we will fall, but to show us how strong the Lord can be in our lives. Jesus loves you; He will not allow the enemy to snatch you out of His hand. (John 10:29

- o   Ministry to children:  Matthew. 8:5-13; 9:18, Mark 9:14-29, Mark 5:22, Luke 8:41

# SAMPLE PRAYERS FOR YOUR FREEDOM[147]

## Prayer #1 for Freedom[24]

Dear Heavenly Father,

I renounce Satan and all the spiritual forces of wickedness that rebel against God.

I renounce the evil powers of this world which corrupt and destroy the creatures of God.

I renounce all sinful desires that draw me from the love of God through Jesus Christ.

I turn to the one, true Jesus of Nazareth and accept Him as my Savior, Lord, and King.

I put my whole trust in Jesus' grace and love for me.

I promise to follow and obey Jesus Christ all the days of my life as His disciple.

In Jesus' Name,

Amen

*Repent, then, and turn to God, so that your sins may be wiped out, that times of refreshing may come from the Lord.*
*Acts 3:19*

*Jesus Christ died for every sin in your life.*

---

24   The Lord's Prayer:  "'Our Father in heaven, hallowed be Your name. Your kingdom come, Your will be done, on earth as it is in heaven. Give us today our daily bread.  And forgive us our debts, as we also have forgiven our debtors. And lead us not into temptation, but deliver us from the evil one (Matthew 6:9-13).

## Prayer #2 for Freedom

Lord Jesus Christ, I come to You today, in need of You as my Deliverer.[25] I believe that You died on the Cross for my sins and rose again from the dead. You redeemed me by Your blood, shed at the cross of Calvary, saved me from my sins and I belong to You. I thank you, Lord Jesus, for Your shed blood, which cleanses me from all sin.[26] I want to live only for You.

I confess *all* of my sins, each one, known and unknown (Take time to confess each sin. This may take several sessions of prayer to do). I repent[27] of each one. Help me to turn from them, Jesus Christ. I renounce[28] any seeming benefit I may have received from these activities.

Forgive me for these sins now and cleanse me from them with Your blood. I repent of any way I have sinned or opened the door to the Devil, who is the enemy of my soul. I renounce Satan, all his works, and all of his workers.[29]

I forgive[30] others just as I want You to forgive me. I choose to release the same mercy that You show to me to others that have hurt me. I receive Your forgiveness and cleansing.

I call upon You now, Lord Jesus, as my Deliverer. Deliver me and set me free.

I ask You Holy Spirit to fill me with Your wonderful presence and Your divine love. Strengthen me in my mind, will, and emotions. Help me to be a follower of Christ.

All this I do in the name, and on the authority, of Jesus Christ of Nazareth.

Thank You, Lord Jesus.

---

25  6:13 "And lead us not into temptation, but deliver us from evil: For Thine is the king-dom, and the power, and the glory, forever. Amen."

26  1 John 1:7-9 But if we walk in the light as He is in the light, we have fellowship with one another, and the blood of Jesus Christ His Son cleanses us from all sin. If we say that we have no sin, we deceive ourselves, and the truth is not in us. If we confess our sins, He is faithful and just to forgive us our sins and to cleanse us from all unrighteousness.

27  Repent is defined as "to turn from sin and dedicate oneself to the amendment of one's life" *www.merriam-webster.com.*

28  Renounce is defined as "to give up, refuse" *www.merriam-webster.com.*

29  James 4:7 tells us "Submit yourselves, then, to God. Resist the devil, and he will flee from you."

30  "For if you forgive other people when they sin against you, your heavenly Father will also forgive you. But if you do not forgive others their sins, your Father will not forgive your sins." Matthew 6:14, 15.

> I declare that You, God, are good and
> that Satan and his demons are evil.[148]

In this next section read through each category and mark anything that you have been or are currently involved with. Then admit that these are wrong and turn away from your involvement in them. Make a clean break from these sins.

For example: "Lord, I admit that I have committed adultery. I have sinned against my wife, and I have sinned against You. I repent and turn from this sin that I have committed, and I ask You to forgive me for it. I voluntarily send the spirit of adultery away and I break its power in my life in the name of Jesus."

# POSSIBLE SPECIFIC SINS

(Where they apply)

I admit, turn away from, and ask forgiveness for:

### *Spirit of Lust, Perversion and Beastiality*[31]

Child Abuse

Molestation

Incest

Masturbation

Pornography

Filthy Mindedness

Satanic Ritual Abuse/Occult Activity

Ritual Molestation

Rape

Sodomy

Homosexuality & Lesbianism

S & M (Sado-Masochism)

Secrets, Secrecy

Ask God to bless you with the opposite spirit: the Spirit of God,

Holiness and Truth

---

31    The Lord has mingled a perverse spirit in her midst... Isaiah 19:14; Their deeds do not permit them to return to their God. A spirit of prostitution is in their heart; they do not acknowledge the Lord. Hosea 5:4.

### Jealousy[32]

Jealousy

Murder

Revenge and Spite

Cruelty

Coveting

Hatred

Anger & Rage

Violence

Unforgiveness

Ask God to bless you with the opposite spirit: the Love of God[33]

### Spirit of Prostitution[34]

All unfaithfulness

Adultery

Fornication

Prostitution

The love of money

The love of control

The love of power

Idolatry

Ask God to bless you with the opposite spirit: the Spirit of God, and Holiness

---

32  For jealousy is a husband's fury; therefore he will not spare in the day of vengeance. Proverbs 6:34.

33  "If I speak in the tongues of men or of angels, but do not have love, I am only a resounding gong or a clanging cymbal. If I have the gift of prophecy and can fathom all mysteries and all knowledge, and if I have a faith that can move mountains, but do not have love, I am nothing. If I give all I possess to the poor and give over my body to hardship that I may boast, but do not have love, I gain nothing. Love is patient, love is kind. It does not envy, it does not boast, it is not proud. It does not dishonor others, it is not self-seeking, it is not easily angered, it keeps no record of wrongs. Love does not delight in evil but rejoices with the truth. It always protects, always trusts, always hopes, and always perseveres. Love never fails." 1 Corinthians 13:1-8a.

34  They do not direct their deeds toward turning to their God, for the spirit of harlotry is in their midst, and they do not know the Lord. Hosea 5:4 NKJV.

## *Stronghold of Death*[35]

Abortion

Death

Destruction

Ask God to bless you with the opposite spirit: the Spirit of God,

and Abundant Life[36]

---

35   The last enemy to be destroyed is death. 1 Corinthians 15:26.
36   The thief does not come except to steal, and to kill, and to destroy. I have come that
they may have life, and that they may have it more abundantly. John 10:10 NKJV.

# A FINAL OPPORTUNITY
## An Open Letter to Oppressors and Perpetrators
## of Suffering and Injustice

What you are engaged in is a violation of human life. You are causing severe, possibly irreparable, damage to the person you oppress. Through your heinous actions you have destroyed their spirit, their soul, and their body, robbing them of the freedom, sanctity, and dignity with which their Creator endowed them.

I feel compelled to warn you that though I have many ideas of how to punish you, none can compare with the judgment God Himself has prepared for you if you persist in your oppression of others. Incredibly, you have a marvelous and almost unbelievable opportunity to surrender to God, to repent of and turn from your oppressive actions, and to receive Jesus Christ, the Lamb of God, who bore the wrath of God for all who turn from their wicked ways, and accept and follow Him. For it is only through the Cross of Christ that a just God is able to forgive sin without denying justice.

However, should you choose to continue in your current path, make no mistake, you will surely die and bear the full weight of God's wrath, for He is righteous and just. And in your eternally reprobate condition you will suffer incomprehensible torment for the ages to come, without end. On the day of judgment and perdition of ungodly men (2 Peter. 3:7), when "we must all appear before the judgment seat of Christ" (2 Corinthians 5:10), these very words will testify against you, and you will know for all eternity that your path of destruction was avoidable and that you alone are to blame for the judgment you bear.

Therefore, I pray for you, as Jesus instructed us to pray for our enemies. But I don't pray that God would overlook your despicable actions. Rather, I pray, with trembling in my heart, that God, in His kindness, would lead you to repentance (Romans 2:4), and that you would come to your senses before you stand face to face with the eternal Father of all those you defiled through your self-centered lust for power. He is the God who said, "For jealousy is a husband's fury; therefore He will not spare in the day of vengeance" (Proverbs 6:34). "Do not be deceived, God is not mocked; for whatever a man sows, that he will also reap" (Galatians 6:7). I can only fathom what the bowels of hell hold in expectation for you, should you refuse God's offer of mercy (see Isaiah 14:9). But if you turn from your life of sin and oppression and call upon the living God, He will make you a new creation and give you His peace, for you were "created to be like God in true righteousness and holiness" (Ephesians 4:24).

Benjamin Nolot
Founder of Exodus Cry[149]
www.exoduscry.com
www.nefariousdocumentary.com

# ACKNOWLEDGMENTS

When I embarked on this writing journey, I had no idea of the beautiful team our Lord was putting together. People joined us from our own backyard, so to speak, here in the state of Missouri. Later, our work led us farther into the USA and then out to other nations. I love the way our Lord works; and of course, the topic is that large.

Many times our Lord led me with cords of human kindness through what I felt was a very difficult assignment. I felt His presence, and at times even His joy, as I wrote or prepared to write each time. So, to Him I offer my deepest thanks and gratitude.

Every contributor has touched my own heart in a deep way. I co-labored (a labor of love and joy) with God's hand-chosen co-author Jackie Macgirvin with *www.ChristianBookDoctor.com*. Jackie has a very good work ethic, so our book project went through in a timely manner. Jackie is an experienced author and is also an excellent creative writer. She brought in many ideas, contributions, and suggestions. I felt our work was fresh and alive. I *thoroughly* enjoyed working with her all the way through the book work, with all its twists, turns, and changes!

Armistead Blunda joined me in the editing/proofreading arena in our first book together. She is a great gift of God, brings great joy to me, and excellence to our work. When she had health problems during this project, I felt like I was walking with a limp. She is that valuable.

So many outstanding authors, contributors and endorsers that have come from my IHOPKC Community. I stand in appreciation of my senior pastor Mike Bickle, for his love, integrity, and diligence in and to the Word of God. He has taken a bold and faithful stand for Biblical truth. It is a privilege to be part of the IHOPKC community.

I want to specifically give thanks to Hal Lindhardt, Bob Sorge, Benji Nolot, Laura Marion, Hope City participants, Chi and Lilian Ukpai to name a few of the IHOPers who worked alongside us. Others who contributed so extravagantly were Glenn Miles, Ph.D., Patricia King, Darrell Brazell, Todd Morrison, Dale Jimmo, Linda Valen, Jonathan Daugherty, Bill Corum, Jeff Gay and David Hairbedian, Lee Harms, Richie and Heather Cruise, Gary Hardy. I want to extend appreciation to Emily Lam (Hong) for her artwork.

I am indebted to the intercessors who prayed over this book project. How many times I felt their prayers carry us through!

> My heart is stirred by a noble theme
> as I recite my verses for the King;
> my tongue is the pen of a skillful writer.
>
> Psalms 45:1

To God be the glory, and may this book bring Him much pleasure.

## *J. L. Matthews*

# BOOKS AND RESOURCES

**Allender, Dr. Dan B.** *A WOUNDED HEART -- HOPE FOR ADULT VICTIMS OF CHILDHOOD SEXUAL ABUSE.* (Colorado Springs: NAVPRESS, 1995).

> Dr. Allender exposes the rage, fear, and confusion locked deep inside every victim. Offering guidance in the midst of this confusion, he shows that there is hope for the wounded heart.

**Brazell, Darrell.** *NEW HOPE FOR SEXUAL INTEGRITY.* (Lawrence: 2012). *www.newhope4si.com)*.

> *New Hope for Sexual Integrity*, is a Christian manual for those recovering from sexual addictions. This groundbreaking recovery manual provides insights gleaned from Scripture, a broad base of recovery literature, brain science and over eight years of working with individuals wrestling with lust, pornography, sexual bondage, and addiction.

> *New Hope for Sexual Integrity* provides clear direction and proven recovery principles for individuals and groups. Darrell writes out of his own journey of recovery and uses many personal stories and applications to which most men can relate. He writes (and speaks) from the perspective of a new individual coming to him for help. Darrell addresses the core issues spiritually, behaviorally, and psychologically that are at the foundation of sexual bondage and addiction. Darrell is an author, teacher, and pastor of a local church. You can find many materials and resources on his Web site listed above, including his invaluable manual *New Hope for Sexual Integrity*.

**Carnes, Patrick J. Ph.D.** *A GENTLE PATH THROUGH THE TWELVE STEPS: THE CLASSIC GUIDE FOR ALL PEOPLE IN THE PROCESS OF RECOVERY.* (Center City: Hazelden, 2012).

> "The twelve steps tap into the essential human process of change and will be regarded as one of the intellectual and spiritual landmarks in human history."--Patrick Carnes

> It was out of his reverence and respect for the wisdom and therapeutic value of the Twelve Steps that Carnes wrote A Gentle Path through the Twelve Steps, now a recovery classic and self-help staple for anyone looking for guidance for life's hardest challenges. -- Unknown.

**Celebrate Recovery.** (CelebrateRecovery.com) is a biblical and balanced program that helps overcome hurts, hang-ups, and habits. It is based on the actual words of Jesus rather than psychological theory. It was designed as a program to help those struggling with hurts, habits and hang-ups by showing them the loving power of Jesus Christ through a recovery process. Celebrate Recovery is now in over 20,000 churches worldwide!

**Eldredge, John.** *WILD AT HEART.* (Nashville: Thomas Nelson, 2001).

> This best-seller invites men to recover their masculine heart, defined in the image of a passionate God. Also see *Wild at Heart Field Manual* by the same author.

**Genung, Mike.** *100 DAYS ON THE ROAD TO GRACE: A DEVOTIONAL FOR THE SEXUALLY BROKEN.* (Colorado Springs: Blazing Grace Publishing, 2013).

> For those who want freedom from porn or sex addiction. This book builds on *The Road to Grace; Finding True Freedom from the Bondage of Sexual Addiction*, and takes the reader into new territory.

**Hawkins, Diane.** *MULTIPLE IDENTITIES -- UNDERSTANDING AND SUPPORTING THE SEVERELY ABUSED.* (Grottoes: Restoration in Christ Ministries, 2009).

Designed to bring understanding and support to survivors of severe childhood sexual abuse -- especially those who suffer from Dissociative Identity Disorder (DID), as a result of sexual or ritual abuse.

**Hundley, Shelley.** *OVERCOME ANGER, REJECT BITTERNESS, AND TRUST IN JESUS WHO WILL FIGHT FOR YOU.* (Lake Mary: Charisma House Book Group, 2011).

The daughter of American missionaries, Shelley Hundley was born in Colombia, and grew up on the campus of a seminary that trained leaders to serve in what was one of the most violent nations in the world. After suffering abuse at the hands of a minister in the community, she turns from God, angry and confused that He could allow this to happen.

In A Cry for Justice, Hundley uses her story as a backdrop to show how she found healing from the pain, guilt, and shame of the abuse she endured as a child and how she came to know Jesus in a new way: as a righteous judge who fights for His people and takes upon Himself the burden of our injustices and pain.

The story of Shelley Hundley's journey from bitter atheist to wholehearted lover of God is unique. Yet what she learned on this journey is relevant to every person who has ever been hurt and has silently wondered, "Who will fight for me? Who can make the wrong things right?"

**Laaser, Dr. Mark.** *HEALING THE WOUNDS OF SEXUAL ADDICTION.* (Grand Rapids: Zondervan, 2004).

This book offers a path that leads beyond compulsive thoughts and behaviors to healing and transformation. Sensitive to the shame of sexual addiction without minimizing its sinfulness, Dr. Mark Laaser traces the roots of the problem, discusses its patterns and impact, and maps out a biblical approach to self-control and sexual integrity. Previously titled *Faithful and True*, this revision includes an all-new section that deals with sexual addiction in the church. Other important changes reflect cultural trends, and current research, placing a greater emphasis on spiritual growth. This book also addresses the unique needs and issues of female sex addicts.

**Lehman, Dr. Karl**. *THE IMMANUEL PROCESS. (www.kclehman.com).*

> This is one of the most effective tools for dealing with trauma. Dr. Lehman is a board-certified psychiatrist who has developed an approach that leads people into healing prayer by connecting to Jesus Christ, who comes as "God with us." (See: "Brain Science, Emotional Trauma, and the God Who is With Us~Part 1" available on his site).

**Macgirvin, Jackie.** *ANGELS OF HUMILITY - A NOVEL.* (Shippensburg: Destiny Image, 2011).

> Look into the spirit realm where angels and demons interact with two average Christians, Paul and Sarah. By watching them you will understand what goes on in the unseen spiritual realm. If you do not realize you are caught in a spiritual battle, you are easy prey. What are the strategies and schemes of the enemy against you, and what weapons can you use to defeat them? How can you enforce the victory that Jesus has already provided for your defense?

**Malarek, Victor.** *THE JOHNS: SEX FOR SALE AND THE MEN WHO BUY IT.* (New York: Arcade Publishing Inc., 2009).

> Victor Malarek demonstrates that prostitution is a pandemic that is destroying more lives worldwide than ever before. An award-winning investigative journalist, Malarek has produced a sort of sequel, or companion, to 2004's *The Natashas*, which examined the flourishing sex trade (and its adjunct, human trafficking) in post-Soviet Eastern Bloc countries. Here he looks at the "demand side": the men who rent them. The resulting investigation of johns in Europe, Asia, North America, and Australia provides as disgusting a catalogue of venality, cruelty, and turpitude as you could imagine.

**Malone, Dr. Henry.** *SHAME, IDENTITY THIEF.* (Irving: Vision Life Publications, 2006).

> Shame told me that there was something fundamentally wrong with me and that everyone knew about it. I willingly accepted that I *did* wrong because somehow, I *was* wrong. I did not make

a mistake; I *was* a mistake. Life then became a task to do rather than a journey to enjoy. I had bought into the lie. As you read SHAME:Identity Thief, you will find the principles that will give you the keys to unlock and break free from shame. You will then be able to enjoy living in the light - living without a mask.

**Prince, Derek.** *EXPLAINING BLESSINGS AND CURSES.* (Kent, United Kingdom: Derek Prince Ministries, 1994).

Life's trials and triumphs can seem accidental. One person may feel that life is a constant struggle in which pitfalls abound and someone seems out to get him. Another may feel that every day is a gift from God with special blessings just for her. That's because forces are at work in our lives: the blessings of a loving God or the curses of our spiritual adversary. The message in this booklet can be of tremendous help to many people. It can change lives, communities, churches, and even nations.

**Rivers, Francine.** *REDEEMING LOVE -- A NOVEL.* (Colorado Springs: Multnomah Books, 1997).

California's gold country, 1850. A time when men sold their souls for a bag of gold and women sold their bodies for a place to sleep. Angel expects nothing from men but betrayal. Sold into prostitution as a child, she survives by keeping her hatred alive. And what she hates most are the men who use her, leaving her empty and dead inside. Then she meets Michael Hosea, a man who seeks his Father's heart in everything. Michael obeys God's call to marry Angel and to love her unconditionally. Slowly, day by day, he defies Angel's every bitter expectation, until despite her resistance, her frozen heart begins to thaw.

But with her unexpected softening comes overwhelming feelings of unworthiness and fear. And so Angel runs. Back to the darkness, away from her husband's pursuing love, terrified of the truth she no longer can deny: Her final healing must come from the One who loves her even more than Michael does...the One who will never let her go.

A powerful retelling of the book of Hosea, *Redeeming Love* is a life-changing story of God's unconditional, redemptive, all-consuming love.

**Roberts, Dr. Ted.** *PURE DESIRE: HOW ONE MAN'S TRIUMPH CAN HELP OTHERS BREAK FREE FROM SEXUAL TEMPTATION.* (Ventura: Regal Books, 1999).

> There is a battle going on. Millions of victims are trapped in the struggle of sexual addiction with no apparent way out. *Pure Desire* is the answer to this desperate cry for help from men and women who have tried to build sexual holiness into their lives and failed... and failed...and failed. This book is also for the shattered souls of mates who are puzzled, shamed, and wounded by their husband's or wife's sexual bondage and secret life. And, this book is for the Church to come alongside those who have come to them for help.
>
> Here is hope for establishing healthy personal boundaries with proven, practical applications to claim Christ's healing power and presence, perhaps for the first time.... Pure Desire is an anchor amid rough waters and the offer of a new appreciation for Christ's healing power and presence. The time is now to begin walking in victory and help others to do the same. Learn how to tackle this issue with confidence, clarity, and biblical perspective.

**Sorge, Bob.** A COVENANT WITH MY EYES. (Kansas City: Oasis House, 2013).

> This book sounds a bold call to the highest consecration in our sexuality. Get ready for a unique book that is apprehending, prudent, and empowering. Based on Bob's own experience with Job 31:1, this book extends an invitation to actually make a covenant vow before God with our eyes. Written for all ages, men and women alike, this book excavates from the ancient spirituality of the book of Job the master key to consecration and illuminates its relevance to us today. The careful writing style will make you feel safe recommending this book even to teens.

**Springle, Pat.** *FREEDOM BEGINS HERE. (DEVOTIONAL JOURNAL)* (Miami Shores: Murray Media, 2008).

> In these 30 days, you will realize that you have choices every minute

of every day to focus your thoughts on what is good and right and wholesome, or to let your mind drift back into the swamp of sexual sin. Make the effort. Your family, your friends, your God and sooner or later you, too, will be delighted you did. *Freedom Begins Here* is challenging Christians everywhere to join a bold movement to break the chains of pornography in our culture. Experience this 30-day journey of hope, direction and change.

**Weiss, Dr. Douglas**. *SEX, GOD AND MEN: A GODLY MAN'S ROAD MAP TO SEXUAL HELP.* (Lake Mary: Siloam, 2002).

Finally, an encouraging message for men who want to be sexually successful. What is sexual success? It's having a three-dimensional (body, mind and spirit) connection to your spouse alone that grows increasingly more fulfilling throughout your lifetime together. God is not against sexual pleasure in your marriage. In fact, He created it. Dr. Douglas Weiss has clearly and creatively outlined practical, doable suggestions and principles that will help you enjoy your sexuality as God intended.

**Wilder, Jim.** *LIVING WITH MEN.* (Pasadena: Shepherd's House Inc., 2004).

*Living with Men* combines the latest science and the oldest wisdom for training the control center in a man's brain for relationships. Immature men create leadership, parenting and relational failures, leaving deep pain in children, couples, families, churches, communities, and themselves. Called a "life changing book."

**XXXchurch.com**

This is your online resource to fight porn and sexual addiction? XXXchurch offers addiction resources for men, women, parents, and couples highlighting awareness, prevention, and recovery. They feature weekly articles on how to conquer difficult issues, as well as porn accountability and filtering software. Free sexual addiction test. The #1 Christian porn site designed to bring awareness, openness and accountability to those affected by pornography.

**XXXFold/Facebook.com**

This site and ministry is dedicated to working with men who have found themselves caught in an addiction cycle that seems to be out of control and unmanageable. The first thing we want you to know is, you are not alone.

"Perhaps you stumbled upon this site in search of porn. Well, there is no porn here, but this very well could be your first step towards a porn-free life." Facebook.com/XXXFold

**YouTube.com/The Power of Forgiveness**

This is a very powerful video on forgiveness. Full of truth about the difficulty of forgiveness, it tells us: "When deep injury is done to us, we never recover until we forgive . . . Forgiveness does not change the past, but it enlarges the future."

# END NOTES

1 Psalms 42:5 NASB

2 Maria Robinson, [http://www.goodreads.com/quotes/186119-nobody-can-go-back-and-start-a-new-beginning-but] 9/3/13.

3 Sadism and Masochism-The practice of using pain as a sexual stimulant. http://www.urbandictionary.com/ Bondage and Domination-Referring to the practice of restraining a sexual partner and then asserting one's control over them through a variety of methods http://www.urban-dictionary.com.

4 Lehman, Dr. Karl. *THE IMMANUEL PROCESS* ("http://www.kclehman.com" www.kclehman.com).

5 *NEW HOPE FOR SEXUAL INTEGRITY* New Hope Fellowship www.NewHopeLawrence.com.

6 Internet Safety 101. Pornography Statistics, *[http://www.internet-safety101.org/Pornographystatistics.htm]*.

7 Top Ten Reviews. Internet Pornography Statistics. http://internet-filter-review.toptenreviews.com/internet-pornography-statistics-pg4.html.

8 George Collins, *Breaking the Cycle: Free Yourself from Sex Addiction, Porn Obsession, and Shame* (Oakland; New Harbinger Publications), 19.

9 George Collins, *Breaking the Cycle: Free Yourself from Sex Addiction, Porn Obsession, and Shame* (Oakland; New Harbinger Publications), 19.

10 http://marriage.about.com/cs/sexualstatistics/a/sexstatistics.htm.

11 http://www.protectkids.com/effects/justharmlessfun.pdf.

12 http://fightthenewdrug.org/i-am-not-porn/#sthash.PP7w1d7Z.dpbs.

13 Darrell Brazell http://newhopelawrence.com/recovery.html.

14 Todd Morrison UntoLife; Mechanicsburg, PA;Phnom Penh, Cambodia.

[15] Fight the New Drug, "Eight Girls, One Message: I AM NOT PORN," [http://fightthenewdrug.org/i-am-not-porn/#sthash.PP7w1d7Z.dpbs].

[16] Darrell Brazell  http://newhopelawrence.com/recovery.html.

[17] http://fightthenewdrug.org/gq-magazine-10-reasons-why-you-should-quit-watching-porn/#sthash.IAW4W0Oq.dpuf.

[18] https://www.psychologytoday.com/basics/dopamine.

[19] http://fightthenewdrug.org/porn-changes-the-brain.

[20] http://fightthenewdrug.org/porn-changes-the-brain/#sthash.LrYA1h1q.dpbs.

[21] Darrell Brazell  http://newhopelawrence.com/recovery.html.

[22] http://www.theguardian.com/commentisfree/2014/oct/14/age-of-loneliness-killing-us.

[23] http://www.huffingtonpost.com/johann-hari/the-real-cause-of-addicti_b_6506936.html.

[25] Nicole Nichols, "4 Good Reasons You Should Pair Up to Work Out," [http://www.sparkpeople.com/blog/blog.asp?post=4_good_reasons_to_exercise_with_a_buddy].

[26] Bridges, A. J., Bergner, R. M., and Hesson-McInnis, M. (2003). Romantic Partners' Use of Pornography: Its Significance for Women. *Journal of Sex and Marital Therapy* 29, 1: 1–14; Schneider, J. P. (2000). Effects of Cybersex Addiction on the Family: Results of a Survey. *Sexual Addiction & Compulsivity* 7, 1 and 2: 31–58.

[27] Steffens, B. A. and Rennie, R. L. (2006). The Traumatic Nature of Disclosure for Wives of Sexual Addicts. *Sexual Addiction & Compulsivity* 13, 2 and 3: 247–67; Wildmom-White, M. L. and Young, J. S. (2002). Family-of-Origin Characteristics Among Women Married to Sexually Addicted Men. *Sexual Addiction & Compulsivity* 9, 4: 263–73.

[28] Bergner, R. and Bridges, A. J. (2002). The Significance of Heavy Pornography Involvement for Romantic Partners: Research and Clinical Implications. *Sex and Marital Therapy* 28, 3: 193–206. - See more at: http://fightthenewdrug.org/porn-hurts-your-partner/#sthash.2fTy5Gv7.dpuf.

[29] http://fightthenewdrug.org/i-am-not-porn/#sthash.PP7w1d7Z.dpbs.

[29] http://fightthenewdrug.org/i-am-not-porn/#sthash.PP7w1d7Z.dpbs.

[30] Layden, M. A. (2010). Pornography and Violence: A New look at the Research. In J. Stoner and D. Hughes (Eds.) *The Social Costs of Pornography: A Collection of Papers* (pp. 57–68). Princeton, NJ: Witherspoon Institute; Ryu, E. (2004). Spousal Use of Pornography and Its Clinical Significance for Asian-American Women: Korean Women as an Illustration. *Journal of Feminist Family Therapy* 16, 4: 75; Shope, J. H. (2004). When Words Are Not Enough: The Search for the Effect of Pornography on Abused Women. *Violence Against Women* 10, 1: 56–72.

[31] Paul, P. (2010). From Pornography to Porno to Porn: How Porn Became the Norm. In J. Stoner and D. Hughes (Eds.) *The Social Costs of Pornography: A Collection of Papers* (pp. 3–20). Princeton, N.J.: Witherspoon Institute.

[32] Pornography Facts. http://poisonographybytes.blogspot.com/2013/04/pornography-facts-and-statistics.html.

[33] http://www.deseretnews.com/article/705395035/Link-between-child-porn-and-sex-abuse-frightening-and-powerful.html?pg=all.

[34] Porn Industry. https://www.shelleylubben.com/porn-industry-stats.

[35] http://en.wikipedia.org/wiki/List_of_countries_by_life_expectancy.

[36] http://www.deseretnews.com/article/705395035/Link-between-child-porn-and-sex-abuse-frightening-and-powerful.html?pg=all.

[37] "http://www.deseretnews.com/author/22686/Emiley-Morgan.html" \t "_blank" Emiley Morgan,"Link between child porn and sex abuse 'frightening and powerful'," [http://www.deseretnews.com/article/705395035/Link-between-child-porn-and-sex-abuse-frightening-and-powerful.html].

[38] http://en.wikipedia.org/wiki/Relationship_between_child_pornography_and_child_sexual_abuse.

[39] National Center for Missing & Exploited Children. Internet Sex Crimes Against Minors: The Response of Law Enforcement. Virginia: National Center for Missing & Exploited Children, 2003.

[40] http://www.deseretnews.com/article/705395035/Link-between-child-porn-and-sex-abuse-frightening-and-powerful.html?pg=all.

[41] EDITORIAL - Child abusers (The Philippine Star) | Updated January 18, 2014.

[42] http://www.protectkids.com/effects/justharmlessfun.pdf.

[43] For further information, please read the chapter called "Dealing

with Dissociation".

[44] http://en.wikipedia.org/wiki/Augustine_of_Hippo#cite_note-26.

[45] http://en.wikipedia.org/wiki/Augustine_of_Hippo#cite_note-Uta-29.

[46] http://en.wikipedia.org/wiki/Augustine_of_Hippo#cite_note-31.

[47] http://www.amazon.com/Confessions-Penguin-Classics-Saint Augustine/dp/014044114X/ref=sr_1_4?s=books&ie=UT-F8&qid=1373509499&sr=1-4&keywords=confessions+of+augustine.

[48] http://www.online-literature.com/saint-augustine/.

[49] http://www.amazon.com/Confessions-St-Augustine-Autobiography-Conversion/dp/1615890254/ref=sr_1_3?s=books&ie=UT-F8&qid=1373509499&sr=1-3&keywords=confessions+of+augustine.

[50] James 5:16.

[51] Justin and Trisha Davis, *Relevant Magazine* April 18, 2013.

[52] *The Help* is a movie that came out in 2011 about African-American maids working in white households in Jackson, Mississippi, during the early 1960s. http://en.wikipedia.org/wiki/The_Help.

[53] http://www.nytimes.com/2012/10/10/sports/ncaafootball/penn-state-sandusky-is-sentenced-in-sex-abuse-case.html.

[54] http://www.huffingtonpost.com/2013/07/18/matt-sandusky-name-change_n_3616042.html).

[55] http://www.childluresprevention.com/research/profile.asp, https://www.bravehearts.org.au/files/Facts%20and%20Stats_updated141212.pdf.

[56] BJS Survey of State Prison Inmates, 1991 reported on http://www.yellodyno.com/Statistics/statistics_child_molester.html.

[57] "http://www.summitdaily.com/apps/pbcs.dll/article?AID=2003305080103" http://www.summitdaily.com/apps/pbcs.dll.

[58] Sarah Tofte http://vigilantantis.wordpress.com/2008/04/28/martin-cusick-repeat-sex-offender-captured-pedophile-absconder/.

[59] Ken Wooden, Rosemary Webb, Jennifer Mitchell, "A Profile of the Child Molester," [http://www.childluresprevention.com/research/profile.asp,].

[60] http://kirkcameron.com/2012/08/penn-state-sandusky-what-about-god/.

[61] http://www.goodreads.com/work/. quotes/16218214-unmasked-exposing-the-cultural-sexual-assault.

[62] https://www.facebook.com/DrGsportspsych/. posts/570517852961438.

[63] http://www.cnn.com/2013/03/17/justice/ohio-steubenville-case/ index.html.

[64] James 5:14,16.

[65] James 5:14,16.

[66] James 1:21.

[67] Psalm 101:3 NKJV.

[68] Contact Transparent Ministries at: www.transparentministries.org/.

[69] Contact Celebrate Recovery at: http://www.celebraterecovery.com/ cr-groups.

[71] Malarek, Victor, *The Johns – Sex For sale And the Men Who Buy It* (New York, Arcade Publishing, 2009) Pg. 102.

[72] STD is defined as "any of various diseases or infections (as syphilis, gonorrhea, chlamydia, and genital herpes) that are usually transmitted by direct sexual contact and that include some (as hepatitis B and AIDS) that may be contracted by other than sexual means." www.merrian-webster. com.

[73] SAGE ("Standing Against Global Exploitation").

[74] Malarek, Victor, *The Johns – Sex For sale And The Men Who Buy It* (New York, Arcade Publishing, 2009) Pg. 258.

[75] http://www.johnhoward.ab.ca/pub/C51.htm#effects.

[76] STD is a Sexually Transmitted Disease while HIV is a Human Immunodeficiency Virus that causes AIDS.

[79] Adapted from a sermon by Chi and Lillian Ukpai, IHOPKC. Used by permission.

[80] Romans 3:23.

[81] Adapted from a sermon by Chi and Lillian Ukpai, IHOPKC. Used by permission.

[82] The product "dynamite" -- derived from the Greek term "dunamis," is the Greek word for "force" or "power." The Greek word "dunamis" also

gives us words such as dynamic and dynamo, and itself probably goes back to the verb dunasthai, "to be able." http://www.answers.com/topic/dynamite.

[83] http://whatheisteachingme.wordpress.com/2010/07/22/sow-a-thought-reap-a-destiny/.

[84] 2 Timothy 2:22.

[85] John 15:5.

[86] Pat Robertson is Chancellor of Regent University, Chairman of the Christian Broadcasting Network, and founder of HYPERLINK "http://en.wikipedia.org/wiki/Regent_University" \o "Regent University" Regent University. He recently accepted the Churchill Lifetime Achievement Award.

[87] Hayford, Litt.D., Jack W. *Spirit Filled Life Bible* (Nashville, Thomas Nelson,  1991) Pg. 2005. We ask you to use caution in cutting off from heavy narcotics. I have seen completed detachment from heavy drugs when in conjunction with 24-hour prayer. This is very successively done in Hong Kong with Jackie Pullenger To's ministry (Saint Stephen's Society).

[88] We ask you to use caution in cutting off from heavy narcotics. I have seen completed detachment from heavy drugs when in conjunction with 24-hour prayer. This is very successively done in Hong Kong with Jackie Pullenger To's ministry (Saint Stephen's Society).

[89] Ephesians 5:22-23.

[90] Ephesians. Ibid.

[91] See Acts 7:58. Later, Saul's name was changed to Paul, reflecting the change in his life after following and becoming a disciple of Jesus Christ.

[92] http://www.covenanteyes.com/blog/.

[93] http://www.albertmohler.com/2013/10/09/how-pornography-works-it-hijacks-the-male-brain.

[94] "Reprinted by permission. Meyer, Julie, *Dreams and Supernatural Encounters* (Shippensburg, PA: Destiny Image Publishers Inc. 2011) All rights reserved.

[95] Abbreviated version of *Love's Not For Sale* -- Helen J. Hicks and Simon Nelson.

[97] Cheryl Taylor- Used by permission.

[98] Tina Turner, released on Capitol Records in 1984. The album "Private Dancer" was Turner's breakthrough after several challenging years of going solo after divorcing husband and performing partner Ike Turner. It is her best-selling album and was responsible for making her globally famous, [www.wikipedia.org/Private_Dancer]. In her autobiography, "I, Tina," Turner revealed several instances of severe domestic abuse against her by Ike Turner prior to their 1976 split and subsequent 1978 divorce, [www.wikipedia.org/wiki/TIna_Turner]. Perhaps these are some of the roots to this melody she wrote and sang, six years after her divorce.

[100] "All You Need Is Love" is credited to Lennon–McCartney. It was first released by the Beatles in July of 1967, [www.wikipedia.org/wiki/All_You_Need_Is_Love].

[101] Chris Altrock, "Fringe: The Fringe Conduct of Peacemaking God Favors," [http://chrisaltrock.com/2010/10/fringe-the-fringe-conduct-of-peacemaking-god-favors.].

[102] *http://voices.yahoo.com/agape-real-love-story-2276550.html.*

[103] www.goodreads.com/author/quotes/838305.Mother_Teresa.

[104] Reprinted by permission.  Hawkins, Diane, *Mutiple Identities: Understanding and Supporting the Severely Abused* (Grottoes, VA: Restoration in Christ Ministries 2009). All rights reserved.

[105] Computers, personal smart phone, iPads, etc …

[106] http://www.blazinggrace.org/cms/bg/pornstats.

[107] Dr. Doug Weiss,  *Beyond the Bedroom*; Health Communications, Inc. 2005.

[108] Mark Kastleman's *The Drug of the New Millenium*; Packard Technologies; 2nd Edition 2007.

[109] Laurie Hall *An Affair of the Mind,* Focus on the Family, First Edition 1996.

[110] Kastleman, *Op. Cit.*

[111] Melody Beattie, *Co-Dependent No More,* Hazelden, 2nd Revised Edition 1986.

[112] www.sexaddict.com.

[113] Walton, Dawn and Brethour, Patrick (September 12, 2011) Boy's Return Hailed as Miracle. The Globe and Mail, pp. A-1, A-6.

[114] Buhler, Rich. *Pain and Pretending* (Nashville, TN Thomas Nelson, Inc., 1991), pg. 35.

[115] https://www.biblegateway.com/resources/ransom-for-many/Chapter-14-Priorities-overturned-Mark-9-30-50.

[116] Dietrich Bonhoeffer, goodreads, [https://www.goodreads.com/quotes/548342-silence-in-the-face-of-evil-is-itself-evil-god].

[117] William Wilberforce, at the close of a speech in House of Commons (1791), as quoted in Once Blind: The Life of John Newton (2008) by Kay Marshall Strom, p. 225 HYPERLINK "http://www.wikiquote.org" www.wikiquote.org web access on 4-17-2013.

[119] Author unknown.

[120] Brazell, *Op. Cit.*

[121] To those who have also been abused: I am sorry. I know and understand the depths of pain caused by others' thoughtless misdeeds. Perhaps you can be the first to break the cycle of abuse for the sake of your children and grandchildren. The Bible gives promises to those who overcome: "I counsel you to buy from Me gold refined in the fire, that you may be rich; and white garments, that you may be clothed and that the shame of your nakedness be not be revealed; and anoint your eyes with eyes salve, that you may see. As many as I love, I rebuke and chasten [discipline}. Therefore be zealous [be eager] and repent. Behold, I stand at the door and knock. If anyone hears My voice and opens the door, I will come in to him, and dine with him, and he with Me. To him who overcomes, I will grant to sit with Me in My throne, as I also overcame, and sat down with My Father in His throne. Revelation 3:18-21, NKJV.

[122] http://www.psych-it.com.au/Psychlopedia/article.asp?id=387.

[123] Brazell, *Op. Cit.*

[124] Proverbs 28:13 The Message Bible.

[125] Henrietta Mears *431 Quotes* (E. L. Doan Ed.). Glendale, CA: Regal Books. 1970 Quotable Christian.

[126] David Livingston, Missionary to Africa. www.preach-the-gospel.com.

[127] Gary Hardy, Used by permission.

[128] "https://www.biblegateway.com/passage/?search=Matthew" Matthew 28:20.

[129] Shelley Hundley, *A Cry For Justice* (Lake Mary; Charisma House, 2011), 54.

[130] Matthew Henry, *Concise Commentary on the Whole Bible*, (Nashville; Thomas Nelson Inc., 1997), 1289.

[131] Helen Hosier, *The Quotable Christian* (Uhrichsville; Barbour Publishing, 1998), 22.

[132] 2 Corinthians. 5:17 (NLT).

[133] The Navigators, [https://www.navigators.org/Tools/Discipleship%20 Resources/Tools/The%20Wheel].

[134] http://www.gotquestions.org/Christian-doctrine-salvation.html.

[135] Brazell, *Op. Cit.*

[136] "Intercessory missionaries" raise their own support to work as full-time missionaries who reach out to others from a lifestyle of prayer and worship. They go from a prayer room to a classroom and then to ministry outreaches and works of service.

[137] Hope City is located in the inner city of Kansas City, MO and works with the homeless, gang members, drug addicts, children, and the poor to bring about change and provide a community where addicts, the fatherless, and the hopeless can belong. Programs include a soup kitchen, a food distribution program, and a day-and-night prayer room. Their goal is to bring each person whose life they touch into a productive, self-managing, and independent lifestyle.

[138] "Enter through the narrow gate. For wide is the gate and broad is the road that leads to destruction, and many enter through it. But small is the gate and narrow the road that leads to life and only a few find it" (Matthew 7:13).

[139] Author unknown.

[140] Augustine of Hippo, goodreads, *[http://www.goodreads.com/ quotes/42572-because-god-has-made-us-for-himself-our-hearts-are]*.

[141] This chapter is excerpted from Bob Sorge's book, *A COVENANT WITH MY EYES.* This book will equip you to make a covenant with your eyes in wisdom and understanding. (www.oasishouse.com).

[142] Hawkins, Diane, *Multiple Identities: Understanding and Supporting the Severely Abused* (Grottoes, VA: Restoration in Christ Ministries 2009), pp. 1-2, 18. All rights reserved. www.rcm-usa.org. Reprinted by permission.

[143] *Ibid*

[144] Lee Harms, *Healing and Deliverance Fundamentals* (King of Glory International Publications, Moravian Falls; 2014).

[145] "From there He arose and went to the region of Tyre and Sidon. And He entered a house and wanted no one to know *it*, but He could not be hidden. For a woman whose young daughter had an unclean spirit heard about Him, and she came and fell at His feet. The woman was a Greek, a Syro-Phoenician by birth, and she kept asking Him to cast the demon out of her daughter. But Jesus said to her, 'Let the children be filled first, for it is not good to take the children's bread and throw *it* to the little dogs.' And she answered and said to Him, 'Yes, Lord, yet even the little dogs under the table eat from the children's crumbs.' Then He said to her, 'For this saying go your way; the demon has gone out of your daughter.' And when she had come to her house, she found the demon gone out, and her daughter lying on the bed."

[146] "Then they came to the other side of the sea, to the country of the Gadarenes. And when He had come out of the boat, immediately there met Him out of the tombs a man with an unclean spirit, who had his dwelling among the tombs; and no one could bind him, not even with chains, because he had often been bound with shackles and chains. And the chains had been pulled apart by him, and the shackles broken in pieces; neither could anyone tame him. And always, night and day, he was in the mountains and in the tombs, crying out and cutting himself with stones. When he saw Jesus from afar, he ran and worshiped Him. And he cried out with a loud voice and said, 'What have I to do with You, Jesus, Son of the Most High God? I implore You by God that You do not torment me.' For He said to him, 'Come out of the man, unclean spirit!" Then He asked him, "What is your name?' And he answered, saying, 'My name is Legion; for we are many.' Also he begged Him earnestly that He would not send them out of the country. Now a large herd of swine was feeding there near the mountains. So all the demons begged Him, saying, 'Send us to the swine, that we may enter them.' And at once Jesus gave them permission. Then the unclean spirits went out and entered the swine (there were about two thousand); and the herd ran violently down the steep place into the sea, and drowned in the sea. So those who fed the swine fled, and they told it in the city and in the country. And they went out to see what it was that had happened.

[147] Annie Schumacher, *Sozo The Nations,* (Amazon Digital Services,

2013)75-106. *www.sozothefoundations.com*;  www.sozothenations.com. Reprinted by permission.

[148] Author unknown.

[149] www.exoduscry.com/ Exodus Cry is built on a foundation of prayer and is committed to abolishing sex slavery through Christ-centered pre-vention, intervention, and holistic restoration of trafficking victims.

Made in the USA
Charleston, SC
29 July 2015